Juliet Bravo

LONGMAN IMPRINT BOOKS

Juliet Bravo

five scripts from the first series
on BBC Television by

Ian Kennedy Martin
Ray Jenkins
Paula Milne

selected and edited by
Alison Leake

 Longman

LONGMAN GROUP LIMITED
Longman House, Burnt Mill,
Harlow, Essex CM20 2JE, England.
and Associated Companies throughout the World.

First published by arrangement with
The British Broadcasting Corporation 1983
Second impression 1983

ISBN 0 582 22103 X

Set in 10/11 pt Baskerville
Printed in Hong Kong
by Hing Yip Printing Co.

'Expectations' will be available for non-theatrical hire on Sony U-matic,
VHS (and possibly Betamax) videocassette formats at a hire charge of
£10 (exclusive of VAT and carriage) from:
BFI Film and Video Library
81 Dean Street
London W1V 6AA
telephone: 01 734 6451

Contents

Introduction

"Once upon a time there was *Z-Cars, Softly, Softly, Hunter's Walk, Dixon* even. They were all just another form of the myth, but at least they showed the police as a service, and not just a bloody force. Now all we show is the crash, the bang, the wallop...More and more, all we produce is the British equivalent of American Junk."

This was the lament of an imaginary scriptwriter in a television play that appeared shortly after the first series of *Juliet Bravo*. These reservations about modern police drama must surely have been written before *Juliet Bravo* came to our screens, for the scriptwriter goes on:

"It isn't only the violence...It's the way we misrepresent. That misrepresentation becomes part of the public expectation. They are conditioned by us to expect that's how families live, how policemen behave, how doctors behave, how everyone behaves. Fifty-minute stereotypes with crash-bang-wallop solutions to all their problems. And we never stop to think about the terrifying blandness of it all."

Juliet Bravo does give us the chance to stop and think. Maybe it's the small-town environment which caught the interest of Ian Kennedy Martin, who devised the series; maybe it's the focus on a woman, which was the seed of the series for the BBC; maybe it's just the present mood of society. Whatever the reasons, the emphasis of this series is different from that criticised by the imaginary scriptwriter.

Take the representation of "how policemen (only men?) behave". Now here is a woman in charge of a police station. Not a wonder woman; indeed, in the words of Stephanie Turner, who played the part of Jean Darblay, a woman who is "nothing particularly glamorous". She is simply a woman doing the same job as a man – no better, no worse. Before *Juliet Bravo*, women in police series were incidental, a decorative part of the

---

* *Jack's Trade* by Richard Harris (ATV)

background. Stephanie Turner once had a small part in *Z-Cars*. She remembers that she was the first policewoman who actually spoke in the series! As a rather flighty character, her only role was to cause a bit of marital trouble among the men at the station. Now we can observe policewomen like Maggie Cullinane and Hannah Maynard moving beyond the sexual stereotype and learning to project themselves with dignity and responsibility. Hannah in particular has to learn that police work is not all glamour and drama.

What about the representation of "how families live"? *Juliet Bravo* offers us the opportunity to watch a couple come to terms with a new life-style. The husband has to cope with the indignity of redundancy, and accept the reversal of traditional roles. Then he starts a new job and they both suffer as their careers conflict. There is no easy solution for Jean and Tom. We see other families resort to the quick, aggressive response to their problems – the Murphys and the Cartwrights, for instance. But we also witness the dreadful misery it brings. *Juliet Bravo* is certainly never "bland".

The imaginary scriptwriter condemned the series he was preparing as "another *Starsky and Hutch* in Downtown Shepherd's Bush...I give them what they want, violence, the lot..." In Hartley the priorities of the police force are clear. The violent end to one case is sorely regretted, not casually dismissed. The crime of two teenagers stealing from an old man, in another episode, is given as much time and attention as the threat of "soccer hooligans". But even more significant is the fact that although the central character is a member of the police force, she is not the focus of every episode. The series paints a very full picture of community life. Is it a misrepresentation of the work of the police? Is it a false picture of the concerns of society today? Is it what we want on our television screens? That's for you to decide.

Alison Leake

Putting a series together

Joan Clark, BBC Script Editor

I am a script editor in TV Drama Series/Serials Department. The idea of a series about a woman police officer was given to me to think about by Graeme McDonald, Head of the Department. He no doubt left it with me because I have accumulated considerable experience of police programmes over the years – from a thirteen-part series called *Scotland Yard* way back in 1960, *Z-Cars* from 1962 onwards, then *Softly, Softly*. All these were factually based programmes, reflecting viewers' interests at the time. In the early 1970s, for instance, there was a move towards racy, jokey, action-packed, punch-on-the-nose cop shows.

But, as with life in general, there has been a pendulum swing in programme popularity. No doubt, some sense of a coming public need to turn away from the hectic and back to the comparatively sedate was what encouraged thoughts of how the ever-popular police series could be adapted to such a change of taste. Police series, of whatever nature, are a handy vehicle for good stories. It seemed to me that a uniformed woman officer of intermediate rank would enable us to explore the widest possible story-area. Also being a provincial myself, and having on the whole worked on shows with a provincial background, it seemed that this might be where to set the series – preferably in the North of England. A contact put me in touch with a woman Inspector, at that time in charge of a "section". After a long chat to her, I reported back to Graeme McDonald and the idea was put on the list of programmes to be considered for the forthcoming season. Fortunately the idea was in Ian Kennedy Martin's head at the same time, and he was invited to devise the series.

My role – or a large part of it, at least – is to create an atmosphere in which writers find it possible, may be even pleasurable, to write. It is not an easy business, writing. In our series there are pretty stringent limitations in the sense that a writer must adhere to realistic police procedure and must also be aware that the programme is transmitted in the early evening to family audiences. Then there are practical limitations: limited film effort, limited studio sets (limited by size of studio), and a limited number of non-regular characters. However, I like to think that limitations stimulate creativity.

When discussing the series with writers, I look for a good balance between crime and human interest. The fact that we portray a compact "section" covering a slightly urban area, with a small police station which has five people on duty at any one shift, seems to encourage a microscopic examination of character, and we can look closely at a very varied assortment of people who, by one means or another, catch the eye of the local bobbies. Our writers are of course encouraged to talk to our police contacts and to see something of the area approximating to the location we see on the screen. They are free to write whatever enthuses them within the framework of the format – providing they are not of course overlapping the ideas of the other writers. It's a matter of them saying what they want to say, rather than us telling them what we want them to say.

Ian Kennedy Martin, who devised the series

I actually investigated the idea of a series about a woman CID inspector thirteen years ago. The time, however, wasn't right then – the TV bosses were not convinced that a police series with a woman as the focus would be popular. Then in the spring of 1979 I had an appointment with Graeme McDonald where I was to promote a series idea I'd had, and which later became *The Chinese Detective*. Graeme McDonald was keen on the Chinese detective idea, but as he felt it would take a little while to get off the ground, would I meanwhile like to think about devising a series around a woman police inspector? I talked to Joan Clark, who had been in contact with a woman inspector, and then went to Lancashire to meet this lady.

Ideas for a series are not much use in themselves until a writer creates for them a different and interesting context, and places within the context a group of characters who can then work out various story situations. When I created *The Sweeney*, the idea of yet another series about the Metropolitan Police was not too exciting until I'd invented Regan and Carter, and a series of conflicts that Regan had with his bosses – all based on observation of a contact I had who was a detective in the Flying Squad.

Soon after arriving in Lancashire and talking to the woman inspector I realised I'd found a context for a new series. It would not be about the CID in a big northern city, its focus would be a non-metropolitan area, and the stories would come out of the life-style and geography of the town in which it was set: a northern town bordered by moors, a town where the recession had arrived in 1929 and you knew it would never recover (somebody told me you can tell when a town is poor – it can't afford to pull down its mill chimneys), but – and this was just as important – a town where you find and enjoy real northern humour and warmth.

The primary aim of the series, of course, was to observe the woman operating in an all-male police world. The inspector I met greatly impressed me. A number of things intrigued me about her. She told me, for instance, that she always cut her own hair, as she had found that nearly every time she sat down under the dryer at a hairdresser the phone would go and her presence be required at some fatal accident or other incident. She added that she always went home first to change into her uniform: "I've got enough trouble establishing who I am at the scene of a crime – the public always ignore me, a woman, and talk to my sergeants. I wouldn't go anywhere in plainclothes." I began to construct the character of Jean Darblay.

There are various components to creating a character. There's some model whom you've observed, and then there's simple invention. When I'm creating my characters, I like to write lists of attitudes they might have. I may never use these but they help me build a picture: what are the characters' attitudes to children, to superiors, to society? What papers do they buy? Do they read? If so, what kind of books? What kind of car do they drive? Once I have their attitudes, then they can start to express individual opinions and become interesting. Once the characters are formed, I know what they will say in any given situation.

As soon as the actress or actor starts working on the programme, she or he will also bring a personality to bear on the characterisation, although usually the character is fully established before the programme starts. I don't see that there should be any real difference in writing dialogue for a man or a woman. When I constructed Jean's attitudes, I felt she'd be more prepared to express her emotions, especially about children in trouble or children being abused. And that helps set some scenes.

It's also a useful device to show a character "going against the grain". Tom does this. It would have been more logical to make Jean's husband an inspector too, especially as there is a belief in the Force that no one outside the job can understand the hours and the work. But I wanted, with the series, to reflect some of the problems of society today – the fact that, for instance, there are so many million people unemployed. Nobody is interested in people who are settled and comfortable. TV programmes have got to look at people who are struggling – like most of society. So Tom is first introduced as recently redundant. Then I thought I'd make life more difficult for Jean. Social workers are after all trying to do much the same job as police, but they are often pulling in different directions from the police. Tom's choice of job makes writing the series more complicated – writers have to find out about social work procedure as well as police procedure, but it makes it more challenging too.

A key point in understanding the series is that I knew, before I started writing it, that it would go out at 7.30 on a Saturday night. As a result, I and the other writers can deal with only a section of the police work that Hartley would cover. But within that work are subjects the public won't have considered before – and that, I hope, makes the stories interesting as well as entertaining.

Ray Jenkins, who wrote one of the episodes

Ian wrote six of the sixteen episodes that make up the first series of *Juliet Bravo*. That meant that other writers were called upon to write the rest. What happens when other writers are called in? The producers through experience have a list: they start with Shakespeare, then they come to Ibsen, and then there's Ray Jenkins! If the first two aren't available, they'll call Ray. "Ray," they say, "we've got this great idea about an underwater Rabbi, or a blind dentist, will you come in and see us?" And I go in.

There are about sixty writers who do the bulk of television writing. The producers know who they can trust to give them a professional job. I think the term "professional writer" is very important here. It does mean someone who'll make him or herself aware of what's being created, will read the other scripts, won't produce something inferior, and will bring in a script on time that fits the bill. In the case of *Juliet Bravo*, it is not for the incoming writer to try to write in Ian's style or to match him, but rather to follow police procedure accurately and to produce a story that is in general sympathy with what Ian is doing. It is a professional responsibility – and ability – not to produce a piece that sticks out like a sore thumb in a series which after all has to look a whole.

As with any series, Ian produces a "format" that gives you the boundaries of the series – the setting, the main characters, what their attitudes are. Joan then explains the other limitations – to do with how many sets you're allowed, how many days filming will be allocated. So, if you like, the scriptwriter is given about 50 per cent of his story already established. Outsiders might think that's very restricting, but in fact it's an interesting exercise, even a challenge. If you think of it in another light, television is my publisher. They publish what I want to write, and I've got half of 50 minutes to say what I want to say. Obviously I appreciate the production problems, but I don't think of myself as a pawn in a producer's hands. I obey the rules – that's the discipline of being professional, but I also try to disturb the format.

Joan knows that she won't have to correct my details about police work. I'm usually right about procedure because I check that very carefully with a police friend; that's me being professional. When the producer, Terry Williams, and I meet to discuss my script, we can straight away discuss the story. In this case, we discussed two possible topics – one was a story about an old lady who kept tinned food in her garage, and the other was about some runaway kids. You can see how I developed the first in line with my own interests. But those ideas were both independent of Ian's format. In a sense I could have put them into any series.

In terms of the format itself, I wanted to present two new features: I wanted to write a funny script for Bentley, and I wanted to see what Jean did when she came home at night. She and Tom had just moved into a new home. I thought they're bound to pull down old shelves and that can produce more comedy, and then you can have a scene with Jean being sexy at home, though not necessarily in bed. Stephanie was terrific;

she's a good actress anyway. That scene shows what I mean by "disturbing the format". It's not a set attitude – you don't really expect your police inspector to come home and flirt – and yet, why not?

Let me tell you what happened with the second story in my script, the sub-plot about the "threat of visiting soccer supporters". The sequence of decisions about the ending demonstrates what goes on between scriptwriter and producer over the mechanics of a script.

I love football, but I do not approve of people going through the streets after a match – or any time – breaking windows or smashing fences. My original script actually had a scene with a crowd of supporters singing their way along a street. But Terry, the producer, decided he didn't have the money to pay for a crowd scene. My attitude was that you can't write about soccer supporters without some appearing, so I went to the other extreme: wrote a scene with just Beck sitting in the station, with his feet up, listening to the soccer commentary! Terry of course agreed that was deadly dull. I persuaded him that he *had* to get some sense of the immediacy of a match, the expectation of a crowd, and suggested a police coach waiting for the crowds to come out of the stadium: a kind of calm before the storm. Then there were problems and expense of hiring a coach. In the end they used a BBC location coach with just the backs of two policemen! The feeling of tension was still achieved. Neither of us felt we'd compromised, and in fact it makes the best sort of ending when the audience is left to anticipate what will happen next . . . plus the feeling that Inspector Darblay, having solved one problem, moves on to the next: it's all in a day's work.

There's often an assumption that if you're writing for a series rather than a "Play for Today", you're not taking it seriously. But I do. After all, I'm only as good as my last script. That 50 minute episode is just as much a sonata form for me – with its own shapes and levels – as any "prestige" play. Audiences shouldn't be so surprised that many of the scripts in a series are very good indeed.

The Police Force

"Juliet Bravo" is the police force radio call sign for Hartley Section, which is the police area covering a small town in a Northern Constabulary. There are CID men attached to Hartley, but they do not feature in these episodes. Before reading the episodes it might be helpful to recognise where individuals fit into the Constabulary hierarchy.

At Headquarters

Inspector Maurice Albert Robins (appears in *Relief*)
Sergeant Walters (of Records Dept) (consulted in *Relief*)

At Sub-divisional level

Superintendent Lake

At Hartley section

Inspector Jean Darblay
Sergeant Joseph Beck
Sergeant George Parrish
Police Constable Roland Bentley
Woman Sergeant Maggie Cullinane (for short attachment in *Family Unit*)
Woman Police Constable Hannah Maynard (just out of 10 weeks at training school, appears in *Expectations*)
Police Constable Ian Shelton (appears in *Relief*)
Woman Police Constable Gilbert (from Juvenile Liaison, appears in *Coins*)

*Inspector Jean Darblay
on duty*

*Jean Darblay off duty
with her husband, Tom*

Jean Darblay with Sergeant Joseph Beck

Jean Darblay with PC Roland Bentley

Shot Gun

Ian Kennedy Martin

The Cast

Inspector Jean Darblay

Sergeant Joseph Beck

Sergeant George Parrish

PC Roland Bentley

Superintendent Lake

Tom Darblay

Maskell

Mrs Maskell

Maureen Maskell

Mrs Porter

Doctor Bowles

Ted Watson

Doctor's Secretary

Det Sergeant Melchett

Mr Porter

Journalist

Dorland

Shot Gun

1 A street in Hartley (morning)

The camera takes us along a narrow, mean Victorian street of two-storey workers' houses with no front gardens. Dustbins can be seen on the pavements. It's raining.
In the town background, we see the outline of a gasometer, and the tall, red-brick, disused chimneys of the old mills. Hartley is a town of twelve thousand people, a few miles from Blackburn, and ten miles north of Manchester.
A "G" registered Cortina drives up the street, pulls in. Rodney Maskell, in his fifties, gets out. We focus on his face. He's looking at the nearest house, and appears grim, dangerous, determined.
He heads to a front door, and bangs on the knocker.

2 The bedroom of the house

Through the net curtains Mrs Madge Maskell sees her husband. She reacts worriedly, and quickly turns to her fourteen-year-old daughter making the bed.
MADGE Maureen, quick. It's your dad. Hide.
Maureen exits.
Rodney Maskell bangs again on the knocker. There's no response, so he bangs on, knowing someone's home. The door is finally opened by Madge.
MASKELL I've come for her.
MADGE You just get out of here. Go away. I'm calling the police.
MASKELL She's coming wi' me.
MADGE No!
MASKELL I'm taking her.
MADGE No!
She slams the door.
Maskell, still grim, turns, moves back to the Cortina. The camera moves in on the Cortina's boot. Maskell opens it, takes out a gun bag, unzips it, and pulls out a 12-bore. He loads it quite openly in broad daylight.

3 The back garden of the house

Madge is moving down a long line of washing, sheets, pillow-cases, clothes, unpegging and gathering them in. Her back is to the house, but she shouts towards it:

MADGE Everything you need for whole weekend. Don't forget toothbrush, toothpaste, homework...

She turns.

Maskell is standing there, the fourteen-year-old by his side, crying silently.

Maskell is pointing the 12-bore at Madge's head.

MASKELL I'm going to kill you.

GIRL Don't dad, Da...

Madge gets down on her knees.

MADGE "Hail Mary, full of grace, the Lord is with thee. Blessed art thou among women and blessed is the fruit of thy womb, Jesus. Holy Mary, Mother of God, pray for us sinners now and at the hour of our death, Amen..."

MASKELL The only reason why I will keep this gun with me, is for you. If you tell the police I have this gun they will come after me. If that happens I will find you wherever you are, and kill you.

Slowly Maskell presses the gun against her throat to emphasise his threat.

GIRL Don't, Dad...

He turns, lifts the 12-bore, fires at a large double bed sheet still on the line, shredding the centre of it. Madge is still on her knees and starts crying.

Maskell takes the girl by her hand and goes off.

4 A road of semi-detacheds in Hartley

We are now in one of a couple of roads of 'Fifties-built houses on the border of the old Mill Town. A Mini comes up the road followed by an Austin 1100. The two cars pull in and brake.

The drivers get out.

The first (from the mini) is Inspector Jean Darblay. There is a description of her later. At the moment she wears an overcoat, so we don't see she's in uniform.

The driver of the 1100 is Tom, her husband, a tall man, with good features, in his early forties.

The two move in through a gate and up to the door of the house. There's a "For Sale" notice in the front garden. Tom tries a couple of keys, and finds the front door key. They enter the hall.

5   Inside the semi-detached house

The camera tracks as they move through the empty ground floor rooms and back to the hall.
Jean is obviously pleased with it.

JEAN What do you think?

TOM Needs money in it.

Jean gives him a look of mock disgust as if that's all he can think to say.

JEAN Bloody hell.

They move up the stairs and enter a bedroom.

JEAN You have no imagination at all, Tom Darblay.

TOM I've got imagination. It's money I lack.

JEAN (*liking the room*) This is us, isn't it...

They move to the landing.

They pass a small room.

TOM This could be my dark room.

JEAN Could we talk about a guest room before a dark room?

They look in on the bathroom.

JEAN Well?

TOM You're mad. £22,000. We've got to find £6,000. I have £1,745 in the bank. £1,200 in the building soc. and £2,000 for the Mini, if we sell it and you have my car. That's it. Apart from my unemployment benefit.

JEAN You'll get a job, Tom.

TOM (*quietly*) I won't get a job. Unless we move. And we can't because of your new promotion.

JEAN You'll get a job, Tom. You've got an interview this afternoon? But don't take a job because you're panicked about not having one.

TOM Buy a house instead.

JEAN Not *a* house, this house.

They look into a large bedroom.

JEAN Subject to survey, I want it. Well?

TOM I've never bought a house at a quarter to nine in the morning.

JEAN Are we going to have it, yes or no? I mean, what the hell's £22,000 in this day and age?

TOM £22,000

JEAN We've looked at seven now.

TOM Okay, Jean.

They come downstairs and pause in the hall.

TOM (*still undecided*) You've got your work to go to.

JEAN This house is £2,000 under-priced. That's worth a quarter of an hour late at work. And I was promised if we meet the price we won't be gazumped.

TOM Gazumped? D'you know how many unemployed there are around here? D'you know how many houses are up for sale?

JEAN This one. Concentrate on this one.

TOM (*shrugging his shoulders*) All right, if you really want it.

JEAN (*giving him a kiss on the cheek*) See you later.

6 The Police Station car park, Hartley

Jean gets out of her car and we have a chance to study her. Inspector Jean Darblay is in her thirties. She's two inches above regulation height, five foot six. She has good features, hair a little short, for practical purposes. (She doesn't have two spare hours a week for the hairdresser.) She's one of the very few women in the UK who run a "section" or its equivalent. That is, she is completely in charge of her area, Hartley Town, and a couple of smaller districts in the eight-mile square patch – and its population of twenty thousand.

She's in charge of it twenty-four hours a day. She has a staff of twenty constables, four sergeants, a clerk, two cleaners, and three CID.

Jean's only been running Hartley two weeks. She's quickly organised a proper parade room and had the sprawling Victorian Police Station meticulously cleaned, probably for the first time in its eighty years' existence.

Hartley was once an all-mill town. It's now a place of mixed fortunes. A third of its population commutes to work in Manchester, a third work in the local industrial estate.

There's a surface suggestion of a reasonable standard of living but also clues that the place is a backwater vulnerable to the state of the nation, to industrial crises, strikes and factory closures.

The Clean Air Act arrived in 1958 but the Victorian granite buildings have not yet been cleaned to celebrate it. The main bulk of Hartley is small two-storey Victorian workers' houses terraced too closely together, a bit like Dagenham.

There's a 'fifties austerity look to parts of the town, especially in the rain, girls shopping in their curlers, Reliant three-wheelers, a shop with the notice "Broken Garibaldi Biscuits, 20p for two pounds".

Jean Darblay is married, no kids. Her husband, Tom, was working as a design draughtsman for a lorry company when it closed. He's been unemployed now six months.

That influences Jean to be close, not remote, from a major problem in the community: unemployment, the threat of it as much as the reality.

7 Hartley Police Station

As Jean heads down the corridor, we take in the painted walls freshly washed, the brass doorknobs gleaming. She passes a couple of her staff.

JEAN Morning, Roland.

PC BENTLEY Morning, ma'am.

Sergeant Parrish, early forties, walks down the corridor carrying a plate on which there is a bacon butty. He tries to hide it.

PARRISH Morning, Inspector.

JEAN Morning, George, quiet night?

PARRISH The Soroptimists*phoned. They say the day best for your lecture would be the sixteenth, and would you confirm.

JEAN Right, George...thanks.

PARRISH And – ma'am – is it right you want parade, nine-thirty?

JEAN Sharp...please.

PARRISH I'll shout the word.

8 Jean's office

Jean's office is large, airy, bare, one desk. There's just two chairs and nothing else but a very floral large carpet square on the linoleum.

Sergeant Beck, in mid-forties, the senior of her four sergeants, is waiting for her.

Beck is a big man, sharp, and definite about everything. Without saying a word or giving a look he manages to convey somehow he's unsure still about the two-week-old rule of a woman at Hartley.

BECK (*gets up*) Morning, boss.

JEAN Morning, Joseph.

---

* Soroptimists: An international federation of professional women who join together to serve their local community.

BECK (*pointing to a file on her desk*) The Houseman file.

JEAN Thank you.

BECK You want a parade at 9.30... We'll be hard put to muster five.

JEAN Five will do.

Beck gives a half nod, half shrug and goes out. Jean takes off her coat.

9 The desk area of Hartley Police Station

Beck crosses the wide room to the duty desk. An old man, Ted Watson, is standing at the desk.

We can also see Sergeant George Parrish, in a glass cubby hole to the street door side of the duty desk.

WATSON (*to Beck*) Oh, morning, Joe.

BECK (*amiable*) Morning, you old devil.

WATSON (*sharp*) Don't call *me* old devil.

BECK I will. You are. (*to Parrish*) George ...she wants it, muster at nine-thirty.

PARRISH (*taking a surreptitious bite of his sandwich*) The call's gone out, Joe.

BECK (*to Watson*) What have you got for us this morning, Ted?

WATSON I'll not tell you and I'll not hang around. My time's valuable. I don't think you appreciate that.

BECK I certainly do, Ted. I always have.

WATSON (*to Parrish*) You said new Inspector would be here at nine o'clock. It's twelve past nine on me digital.

PARRISH Inspector Darblay is here, just give her five minutes to put on her face.

WATSON What d'you mean, *put on her face*?

PARRISH Make-up. The Inspector that's replaced Mr Widdop is a lady, Ted.

WATSON A lady. A bloody woman? I don't believe it.

BECK Then you're almost as surprised as we are.

Jean sticks her head out of the office.

JEAN Sergeant Beck, get me the paper on Tatman and Fielding.

BECK Yes, boss. Oh, ma'am, this gentleman here, Mr Ted Watson, he's been a very useful informant to us over the years, says he has some information for us.

JEAN (*to Watson*) What's that then?

WATSON I've just witnessed a rape, Missis Inspector.

JEAN A rape?

WATSON Yes.

JEAN Any report of a rape, Sergeant Beck?

BECK No, ma'am.

JEAN Come in, Mr Watson.

10 Jean's office

Jean chaperones the old man in.

JEAN Sit down. (*she goes behind desk*) What d'you mean, you've witnessed a rape? We haven't heard of a rape.

WATSON What's your name, missis?

JEAN Inspector Darblay.

WATSON You took over from Mr Widdop. A woman's a bit of a bloody surprise.

JEAN What information d'you have, Mr Watson?

WATSON I want five pounds for it. Mr Widdop always give me five pounds.

JEAN Now just tell me what you've seen.

WATSON Well, I were witness to rape on Tomey Moor. Though I didn't recognise who the assaulting rapist were.

JEAN Could you explain more fully?

WATSON Well, I was out walking. I heard screams in little copse in middle of moor. I went to look. The man runs off. And there's this young girl in terrible state. "I have been raped. I have been raped...Peter did it...Peter..."

JEAN What time was this?

WATSON Do I get five pounds? Then I'll give you my statement.

JEAN Now Mr Watson, I neither know nor care what arrangement you had with my predecessor, but I don't drop fivers easily. If in future you have information about any criminal act, you inform us. (*Jean goes to the door to open it*) Sergeant Beck.

JEAN (*as Beck appears*) Take Mr Watson here to the interview room. See if he'll come up with a statement...otherwise I'll talk to him later.

WATSON (*to Beck*) Here. Look. I told you I'm busy. I'll not sit in any of your rooms. I've me appointment with me acupuncturist...

BECK Come on now. Nice and quiet.

WATSON I won't go in your room. I bloody won't.

BECK Come on, Ted. No shouting or scrapping. This way, young man...

He takes the protesting Watson away.

This is witnessed by sub-divisional Superintendent Lake whom Jean ushers into her office.

LAKE (*indicates the old man*) Local colour?

JEAN I think so. I don't know him. (*She closes the door and goes back to her desk*) Social call, sir?

LAKE Just dropping by. See how you are...

JEAN Thank you, sir.

They sit.

LAKE You've been here a fortnight?

JEAN Exactly fourteen days.

LAKE How are the lot taking it – a woman in charge?

JEAN They're taking their time.

LAKE Yours is an important appointment, Jean. You're one of very few women in England running a whole town like this. Our ladies are usually hived off to Juvenile Bureau, Community Services, HQ Training.

JEAN Yes.

LAKE There're a few around who'd be pleased if you failed in any way. This is still the unliberated North – men are men, so they are at pains to tell you.

JEAN I grew up with that, sir.

LAKE Of course.

JEAN I'm grateful for your advice over the years and your efforts on my behalf. What about tea, sir?

LAKE (*getting up*) No, I'm just here for a nod. I'm to see CID in Manchester. I want a look at the new billiard table.

JEAN Not new, just re-clothed.

LAKE Will it make your team play any better?

JEAN I'll put ten pence on it.

LAKE Next match against our lot?

JEAN Yes, sir.

LAKE You're on.

He goes out.

11 The desk area of the station

Sergeant Beck crosses from the interview room to the desk and speaks to Parrish.

BECK I think Ted might be onto something – it does sound like rape. He's prepared to make a statement and he says he knows who the girl is.

PARRISH What name?

BECK Annabel Porter, Waterloo Estate.

JEAN Parade will only take a minute. Who's available in CID?

BECK Sergeant Melchett's over at Toll Hill...I know he's just leaving a job there.

JEAN Tell him to go to the copse on Tomey Moor – have a quick look round in case the girl's still there. Then come back here. Get someone to bring my car round.

12   The hallway of a maisonette

Mrs Porter, in her fifties, looking harassed, goes to open her front door to find Jean there.

JEAN Hello...Are you Mrs Porter?

MRS PORTER Yes.

JEAN I'm Inspector Darblay. I'm looking for Annabel Porter. *Mrs Porter looks Jean up and down.*

MRS PORTER What d'you want Annabel for?

JEAN Is she here, Mrs Porter?

MRS PORTER She's not.

JEAN Can you tell me where she is?

MRS PORTER Where else – at work! Industrial Estate, Cately's.

JEAN No. We've phoned Cately's. She didn't turn up this morning. Are you sure she's not here?

MRS PORTER Have a look. Please yourself. She's not here.

JEAN Where d'you think she is?

MRS PORTER I don't know. She makes her own life.

JEAN What time was it when you last saw her?

MRS PORTER Seven-thirty about.

JEAN What age is she?

MRS PORTER Sixteen.

JEAN She may make her own life, but as the law is, you're responsible.

MRS PORTER Maybe she took day off, gone shopping.

JEAN Does she know a man called Peter?

MRS PORTER Peter who?

JEAN She doesn't know of any Peter that you know of? Now look, there's the possibility that your daughter might have been attacked.

MRS PORTER Attacked?

JEAN We've had a report in from an old man who was out on Tomey Moor. He may have been mistaken. It may have been another girl, but we have to find your daughter.

We get the impression, as does Jean, that Mrs Porter is holding something back.

MRS PORTER I don't know anything about this. If you've got anything to say about Annabel you must talk to my husband. He's at Johnson's on the Estate. Annabel's not here. I don't know where she is. You have to talk to my husband.

JEAN It's all right, love. We'll sort it out.

Thank you…'Bye…

She turns and goes.

Mrs Porter closes the door behind her.

13 Outside the maisonette

Jean moves down to her car, as a red Ford Escort comes up and pulls in. Jean goes across to it. In the Escort is Detective Sergeant Melchett.

JEAN Did you find anything on the moor?

MELCHETT No, ma'am.

JEAN I still think we've got a rape. If the girl turns up, bring her in with her mum. All right?

MELCHETT Right oh, ma'am …

A message from Sergeant Beck for you. Hartley Park, he's seeing a Mrs Maskell. Says her husband took her daughter off.

JEAN It's going to be one of those days, isn't it?

MELCHETT It looks like it, ma'am.

14 Hartley Park

We see Jean joining Beck and Mrs Maskell. Beck rises from the park bench. He comes to meet Jean and offers her the statement he's taken on a form.

JEAN (*quietly*) What are you doing here?

BECK She wouldn't come to the station.

Jean reads the form, then, followed by Beck, goes over to sit down on the bench with Mrs Maskell.

JEAN Mrs Maskell, you say your husband left home about a fortnight ago…came back this morning and took your child away. You say it was against your will and your child's will. How did he manage that?

MRS MASKELL I don't understand you.

JEAN Well, if your child didn't want to go off with him, did he use force?

MRS MASKELL Use force?

JEAN Threaten you with violence – a weapon, knife, hammer…?

MRS MASKELL (*not meeting Jean's eyes*) No. He didn't. But he said he would be…very angry if I didn't let him have Maureen.

JEAN Well, there's not a lot we can do. No use of force – it's hard to establish that a father has *abducted* his daughter. I'll put a description out to our men, and see if we can pick him and Maureen up. Then you'll have to come into the station and we'll sort things out. You say he made no threats whatever? Do you have any reason to be afraid for her safety?

MRS MASKELL No…

JEAN Allright, Mrs Maskell. And you've no idea where your husband might be living?

MRS MASKELL No – none.

JEAN I want you to contact us immediately if you do hear from him…And next time – we can't take your complaints in a park, you'll have to come down to the station. Come on, Sergeant.

Beck and Jean leave the park.

In the police car. The car is going through the town. At first the pair are silent.

JEAN You happy at your work?

BECK Yes.

JEAN I mean with me?

BECK Oh aye.

JEAN No one will hold it against you if you want to transfer out from under my skirts.

BECK No, boss. I'll give it a try.

JEAN Very generous, I'm sure – you'll "give it a try". Come on, let's talk to Mr Porter.

15   A high hill near the centre of town

On both sides we see low-level Victorian houses. In the background the town spreads out: old mill chimneys, electricity cooling towers, a church in ruins.

Porter strides up the hill. Jean has difficulty keeping up with him. Beck paces them in the white Escort.

PORTER I'm saying nought. I've got a job to get on with Missis Inspector. I'll tell you what happened – but I won't make a statement. I got a phone call at work this morning, my Annabel, she said some young fellow had assaulted her on the common.

She's staying with friends, I don't know where. I phoned me missis and told her to keep her mouth shut about it.

JEAN Annabel might have been the victim of a serious offence.

PORTER Look, woman. We'll know that when she turns up. But this is what her mother and me have worked out. If she has been raped, and as a result of that she's pregnant, we will summons the bastard, if you catch him. If she's not pregnant, we won't.

JEAN What d'you think the law of this land is? Shall I tell you?

PORTER (*angry*) I'll tell you. Law is about courts. I've been to court getting compensation for my foot. They don't even speak the same bloody language as you and me in those courts. And you bet they like a bit of dirt to discuss and get a kick out of. And these bastard lawyers and judges – by the time they're through with it, it's upside down and inside out, and lies. Do you want to put a sixteen-year-old girl through that?

JEAN We don't have a choice. And if we find out that something has happened to your daughter, I think you'll wish you had co-operated.

PORTER If you weren't a bloody woman, I'd belt you one.

Jean signals Beck to pull in. Beck brakes the car, gets out, comes round and opens the passenger door for her.

JEAN Sergeant Beck, there's no reason for you to open a car door for me...

BECK (*peeved*) Yes, boss.

JEAN I want to find that girl and talk to her.

16 A doctor's office

This is a comfortable private-practice office. The camera pans round it to take in Maskell and Maureen and the doctor. Maureen is buttoning up her blouse.

DOCTOR What brought you to see me?

MASKELL I don't believe in the National Health. I don't believe they cure anyone of anything.

DOCTOR Come now, Mister Maskell. That's not what I meant.

MASKELL You've not seen my daughter ill – when she's had her migraines so bad she faints dead away. (*emotional*) And God, I wonder sometimes if she's going to die of it!

DOCTOR I've just given her a quick check-up. She seems reasonably healthy.

MASKELL She's not.

DOCTOR (*studying Maskell's nervousness*) Tell me, is there a stress situation at home?

MASKELL What's that supposed to mean?

DOCTOR Your daughter tells me you blame her mother for her illness.

MASKELL (*snaps*) I do.

DOCTOR Why?

MASKELL Well she'll not get the proper help for Maureen. That's obvious. She takes her down to Doctor Herrick. Saving your profession, he's a bloody useless doctor.

DOCTOR I don't know a Doctor Herrick. Why do you say he's useless?

MASKELL Why? There's a surgery queue a mile long. He gives her a quarter minute and a prescription for nought more'n aspirin. If you want a proper job done in this country now, you have to pay for it, like I'm paying you.

DOCTOR (*patiently*) That's not necessarily true.

MASKELL (*sharp*) Don't argue with me. It's true. It's true.

DOCTOR (*who realises it's Maskell who should be the patient*) Look, migraine in a fourteen-year-old child can be due to many causes. The main ones are stress, or hormonal imbalance.

MASKELL I don't know what that means.

DOCTOR If you'll wait a minute. I'll tell you. Your daughter will have to go through a series of tests.

MASKELL Tests?

DOCTOR To establish possible causes. I'll get my secretary to arrange an appointment for her at County General.

MASKELL Hey, you wait a minute. Are you telling me I've come all the way here and I'm to pay you money for private doctoring only to get sent down to County General, which I could of got for free off Doctor Herrick? I wasn't born bloody yesterday.

DOCTOR (*rising*) You can get out, Mister Maskell, and come back when you've calmed down.

MASKELL (*getting up as well*) Maureen...You'd better watch it, wasting my time...

DOCTOR (*Firm and flat*) Get out of here.

MASKELL Maureen, let's go.

He turns, takes the girl by the hand, strides out, face furious.

The Doctor's secretary comes in.

SECRETARY Doctor Bowles, that young girl wrote this. She asked me to give it to you...

She hands a note to the Doctor who reads it.

17 Outside the doctor's house

We watch Maureen and Maskell come out.

Maskell is clearly boiling with rage. He spots the doctor's car – a Jaguar – with a "Doctor on Call" note behind the windscreen. He goes to his car and helps Maureen into it. He goes back to the Jaguar, looks around for a suitable weapon, spots a large rock in the doctor's front garden.

He goes back inside the doctor's front gate, picks up the rock, staggers out onto the pavement, lifts the rock up and smashes it through the windscreen of the Jaguar.

He goes back to his car, gets in and drives off.

18 The Maskells' kitchen (afternoon)

Jean, Mrs Maskell and Beck are sitting there. Jean reads Maureen's note aloud.

JEAN "My dad will kill her. Tell my mam not to try to get me back or he will kill her. Not to go to Police. I am all right. Maureen Maskell." Now, d'you think your husband would try to attack you – try to kill you?

MRS MASKELL Yes.

JEAN Has he ever attacked you before, physically?

MRS MASKELL No. But you see it's been boiling up – his rage. It's come to a head, I know he is going to do something violent to me or to Maureen.

JEAN Tell me about Maureen's illness.

MRS MASKELL She's always had migraines, since she was a kid

of seven. Lately they've been terrible. He blamed me, blamed our doctor. She's ill but not that seriously. It's him who's really ill.

JEAN Now, who are his friends, love?

MRS MASKELL No one.

JEAN No one has no friends.

MRS MASKELL He has no friends.

JEAN Mrs Maskell, we have to find your husband. You have to tell me where to start looking.

MRS MASKELL Don't you think I've been trying to work that out?

JEAN Well?

MRS MASKELL Nothing. You see he's cunning. No it's worse – sick in the mind.

JEAN Did he ever undergo any treatment?

MRS MASKELL No, it really didn't well to the surface 'till he lost his job. He was always difficult, like there was a great anger in him, always. But from fourteen months ago, when he got paid off, he became worse. It was mainly the money – he's been earning eighty to ninety pounds a week at the mill at Cleckworth – then suddenly the dole. He couldn't cope.

JEAN We're going to take you down to the police station. We can't let you stay here if you're in danger from him. Put a few things in a bag in case it's an overnight stay.

Mrs Maskell exits and Jean gets up.

JEAN (*turning to Beck*) It wasn't just him made redundant, the whole mill closed down. What do you think?

19   A deserted factory (later that afternoon)

The scene comes up on Dorland, opening the metal wire gates. Jean is waiting in the police car with Beck and Melchett.

DORLAND What d'you want? What d'you want?

JEAN I want to talk to you, please – and have a look round. We have a missing girl to find and she might be here.

Dorland stands aside.

Beck drives in and parks in front of the main building. The three get out. Jean instructs Beck and Melchett.

JEAN I'll go inside.

(*to Beck*) You stay here.

(*to Melchett*) You go round to the rear.

BECK There may be a dangerous man in there, ma'am.

JEAN I'll be all right, Joseph.
Melchett heads off round the back of the building.
Dorland comes up to Jean.
JEAN I'd like to check some of these buildings...I'd like you to stay here with the Sergeant. Could you give me the keys...
DORLAND (*handing her a bunch of keys*) How will you know which key fits which door?
JEAN I'll find out. Have you seen an ex-foreman of this plant, Rodney Maskell, around here?
DORLAND No.
JEAN Are you sure?
DORLAND Sure I'm sure. I swear on God's honour.
Jean goes off into the main building.

20 Inside the factory

As Jean moves through what was the main assembly room of the now deserted factory, she spots a patch of light coming from a paint shed.
We enter the paint shed and find Maskell and Maureen behind him. She is withdrawn, reading "Nineteen". Maskell looks up at the sound of a door scraping. He goes over and looks down the empty walled flight of stairs.
MASKELL Dorland? What d'you want? Dorland, come up here. Dorland.
Maskell gets his gun, pulls back the hammer and heads for a stairwell.
MASKELL (*to daughter*) Don't make a sound.

21 The stairs

Jean, still to side of stairs, starts a silent retreat. She needs to get help with Maskell.
As she moves, she retreats into the barrel of his gun.
MASKELL D'you understand what this could do to you, love?
He's standing behind her pointing the gun at her. He's got from the first floor down to the ground floor by some other stairs.
JEAN Put that away.
MASKELL Turn around. Walk. Turn round!
Maureen is coming down the stairs.
MAUREEN Dad, don't do it.

MASKELL Shut up, Maureen.

MASKELL (*to Jean*) Quick now.

JEAN (*calm*) I've got other police officers outside.

MASKELL Aye, and you'll tell them if they make any cheeky moves, you're the one that's for it. Come on, Maureen!

22 The front of the factory

Jean, followed by Maskell and Maureen, comes out of a side entrance of the factory, moves along a wire fence to the front, passing Maskell's old Cortina.

At the front Jean nearly trips over a wire from the broken fence.

Her sudden falling movement brings Maskell's gun barrel thrusting into her back. It's a bad moment for her. Melchett appears from the rear of factory just as Beck moves into view. The two cops stop dead in their tracks at the sight of Maskell, the gun, and Jean.

Maskell, still prodding the gun into Jean, crosses to the squad car and fires at the rear nearside tyre, shredding it. He indicates for Jean to stay put, while he moves back with Maureen to the Cortina.

Dorland meanwhile has come out of the factory.

Maskell and Maureen get into the car, drive off.

JEAN (*to Beck*) Use personal radio. Call Divisional HQ. Ask for firearms officers and dog handlers to attend. I'll phone headquarters.

(*to Dorland*) Where's the phone?

DORLAND Inside.

JEAN Show me, quickly...and I want to talk to you later.

23 The desk area at Hartley Police Station

JEAN Where's Mrs Maskell?

PARRISH Interview room, ma'am.

24 The interview room

Jean enters on Mrs Maskell.

JEAN Mrs Maskell, did you know your husband has a shot gun?

MRS MASKELL Yes.

JEAN D'you have any other information that you're keeping

back from us? D'you know it's an offence not to have given us that information?

MRS MASKELL (*near tears*) Have you found her?

JEAN They were at the mill at Cleckworth. He threatened us with his shot gun. We didn't argue with it. They got away.

MRS MASKELL Is she all right?

JEAN Yes, as far as we could see.

MRS MASKELL Why can't you get my Maureen back?

JEAN Now, Mrs Maskell, I want you to think again. Isn't there a single person he'd turn to in trouble – a relative, or a mate?

MRS MASKELL He had no friends!

JEAN Think about places. Have you always lived in this area? Where have you lived the last ten years?

MRS MASKELL First, council flat, Casimir Road.

JEAN Yes.

MRS MASKELL Then cottage at Elfield.

JEAN When did you leave Elfield?

MRS MASKELL Two years back. Now I know he was right about it. It was a big sprawling cottage, right in the middle of nowhere, all old and ugly. But he loved it.

JEAN Why did you leave it?

MRS MASKELL I couldn't clean it. No proper kitchen. Always some loose roof slates. I said "We have to go modern. I can't take this". Recently I saw a notice on it. It's up for sale again.

We can see Jean has decided that this is where Maskell will go with his daughter.

25 A country lane

Jean, Beck and Melchett can be seen in the Escort. It comes slowly down the lane, cruises past "Marly Cottage" – there is a "For Sale" sign on the front gate.

The three study the cottage.

BECK Shouldn't we wait for some of the circus to arrive from Headquarters?

JEAN We'll have a careful look.

She gets out of the car. The others follow.

The camera tracks with the three as they move cautiously to the gate, turn in, and move up the overgrown path. The front door is padlocked. They go around the side. We see the place from Jean's point of view: the dirty windows, some broken, the sprawling cottage.

The three arrive at the back garden and we also take in the neglected fruit trees and a jungle of long grass...and parked behind a broken greenhouse, the Cortina.

At the moment they spot the Cortina, the three hear a sound, and turn to see the barrels of a 12-bore at the top floor window. It fires.

The whole of the greenhouse dissolves in a cloud of glass. The noise of glass falling lasts for fifteen seconds.

The three pitch themselves forward on to the ground.

They crawl quickly behind a low garden wall and head for the front gate. We see Maskell at the open second floor window, the white-faced girl behind him.

Jean moves swiftly to the Escort, the others following. They drive off down the road.

Jean takes out her personal radio.

JEAN (*into radio*) Inspector Darblay here.

HARTLEY VOICE Yes, Inspector.

JEAN Marly Cottage, Mill Water Lane. Rodney Maskell, fifty-one Burton Road Hartley, discharged shot gun at me. I want firearms and sniper to here. And please put radio on "Talk-through". Over.

HARTLEY VOICE I have all that, Inspector. Out.

26 The front of the cottage

We watch Jean directing various men to take cover, to use dead ground, and to conceal themselves. A dog handler, and his dog move into the trees. The operation is to contain the gunman, but to remain for the moment out of shotgun range and outside Maskell's potential eyeline from the upper floor of the cottage. A private car arrives. Jean intercepts two firearms officers getting out of it. They carry hand-guns.

JEAN I have ten men – and none of them is armed. Where do you want them?

FIRST FIREARMS OFFICER Just keep them well out of the way, ma'am.

They move off – also to take positions well back from the cottage.

JEAN Mrs Maskell?

BECK Wallis is getting her.

JEAN I don't want him to see her yet. Keep her away, and for God's sake tell everybody to be careful.

JEAN (*into P/R*) Inspector Darblay to Superintendent Lake.

LAKE (*dist.*) Superintendent Lake. I'm at Hartley. How is it?

JEAN Serious. He's in this cottage with his daughter and a 12-bore. I've got him contained. Are you coming out, sir?

LAKE'S VOICE I'm on my way. Keep him contained, start a dialogue. We'll sort it out. Over and out.

BECK Is the Chief coming, boss?

JEAN Mr Lake's coming.

BECK (*worried*) Well, I suppose we'd better keep things quietened down until he comes.

JEAN Until he comes, Sergeant, I'm in charge. I'll make the decisions, don't worry.

BECK Yes, boss.

Constable Bentley, from Hartley police station, comes up, putting batteries into a loudhailer.

BENTLEY The batteries were flat. I bought four U-2s, paid with me own money.

JEAN Make out a chitty.

BENTLEY I will, ma'am.

JEAN (*with humour*) Not now, Roland.

BENTLEY No, ma'am.

Jean takes the loudhailer, heads round the back of the cottage.

Beck and Parrish follow.

They get behind the low wall. Jean looks around to see where her men are positioned.

Then addresses Maskell with the loudhailer.

JEAN Rodney Maskell. Inspector Darblay. We're here, quite a number of us, and we have this cottage surrounded. We have two armed policemen out here. Now you've discharged a shot gun, but so far nobody's been hurt. Before somebody does get hurt – and it might be you – you'd better put that gun down and come out.

MASKELL (*at the window*) You bloody woman cop. I'll come out when I want to. My daughter Maureen's with me. Your bloody gunmen won't risk shooting me, and hitting her.

BECK (*coming over to Jean*) Doctor and Mrs Maskell are here.

JEAN Okay. Keep her back. But I'll speak to the doctor.

The doctor comes up just as there's another blast of the shot gun aimed at a tree-top above Jean.

The doctor, Jean and the others get down fast.

Maskell is suddenly seen at the window holding his gun.

MASKELL I'm going to kill myself and my daughter now, unless you get your men away from here. You want me to kill myself and my Maureen? You want to watch it? Free show. I'll do it. The two of us have nothing to live for. Nothing.

JEAN (*into her radio*) Inspector Darblay to Hartley.

HARTLEY VOICE Receiving, ma'am.

JEAN Superintendent Lake still there?

HARTLEY VOICE Left ten minutes ago. He's in his private car, ma'am. On radio, but we don't have contact.

JEAN Phone HQ. See if they can get a traffic patrol to intercept and hurry him up. Situation with armed man developing. He's now threatening life of daughter. We need him here very fast...

27 The bedroom of the cottage

Maskell stands by the window, alternatively looking over garden and then back to Maureen. She's suffering from a migraine and is holding her head.

MASKELL I would not ever harm you, Maureen. The threat's for their benefit. Is the migraine a bad one?

MAUREEN Yes, Dad.

MASKELL (*deeply upset*) Oh, Maureen. Sorry. Sorry. But we will escape. You and me. I will work out a way...

28 The side of the cottage

Jean and Parrish are in discussion.

JEAN (*to Parrish*) What d'you think?

PARRISH I agree with Joe. You've nothing really to lose with her talking to them. I wouldn't like the situation going quiet, giving him time to sink deeper in his mood.

JEAN Get Mrs Maskell.

29 The bedroom of the cottage

Maureen is now half lying on bare floor. Her father is giving her pills.

MASKELL You can take three more of them. They're only aspirin.

MAUREEN Dad. I need water to swallow them.

MASKELL We've no water. I'm sorry. I know they're bitter, but you'll have to chew them to swallow...

21

MRS MASKELL'S VOICE Rodney. Maureen. It's me.
Maskell moves to the window.

30 The garden

Jean, Mrs Maskell, Parrish and Beck are all behind the low wall. Mrs Maskell is speaking into the loudhailer.

MRS MASKELL Rodney. Maureen. Maureen. This is your mother. Listen. I know you love her, Rodney. I know I kept her from you. I won't do that no more. Just come out. Or let Maureen come out. I'll do anything you want.

MASKELL You lying bitch!

He shoots off both barrels of his shot gun, peppering the low wall.

31 The bedroom of the cottage

MASKELL There's a way out of this. If you won't faint on me with your migraine. Will you?

MAUREEN I'm not going to faint.

MASKELL Good. They'll think I'm threatening your life. I'll put the gun to your head and pretend I'm going to shoot you dead or they let us go. That's it. That's how we'll get out.

32 The back garden

From behind the low wall Jean and Beck watch Parrish lead Mrs Maskell away.

BECK (*to Jean*) Mr Lake should be here by now. Shall I try and find out where he is?

JEAN The Super won't save you, Joseph.

BECK It's his experience in situations like this, boss.

JEAN (*coolly angry*) Go away, Joseph.

BECK Yes, boss.

He heads off.

33 The bedroom of the cottage

MASKELL You just walk very slowly in front of me, downstairs,

and out back. I'll be behind you. I'll have my left hand on
your left shoulder, right hand pressing gun into your side.
I'll tell them to get back. Then we walk slowly to the car

MAUREEN Dad, you say you won't shoot me?

*He studies her, a calm trusting look. We realise how much he does love
her.*

MASKELL No, Maureen.

MAUREEN You'd never shoot me?

MASKELL Of course not.

MAUREEN I won't do what you tell me, Dad. And I'm going to
leave this room now, Dad.

MASKELL (*mood change*) But you can't.

MAUREEN You said you won't shoot me.

MASKELL (*sharp*) I'll restrain you…

34 The garden

*An ambulance approaches as Mr Cowley, a local journalist, crawls up
to Jean behind the wall.*

JOURNALIST Afternoon, Ma'am. Have you got a statement for
the press?

JEAN Would you please get back, go away for a moment. I'll talk
to you later.

JOURNALIST Just a few words on the situation.

JEAN My word is…if you don't get back and stay there, you're
obstructing officers in the execution of their duty.

JOURNALIST It's my job to inform my readers, like it's your job
to sort this bloke out.

JEAN Later. Get off with you.

He retreats on knees. Parrish comes up.

PARRISH Ambulance here.

JEAN Any sign of Mr Lake?

PARRISH No.

35 The bedroom

MAUREEN How will you stop me?

MASKELL You will not leave, Maureen.

Slowly she gets up. Slowly he swings round the gun to point it at her.

MAUREEN You said you wouldn't shoot me.

MASKELL No.

MAUREEN You will or you won't?

MASKELL Won't. They will shoot you. They will kill you. They know you are part of me...(*he turns back to the window*) Just give me a moment, one moment. I'm coming to a decision. I don't think we will escape, Maureen. I reluctantly conclude that. But they will not have me to capture. Neither me, nor you, the innocent in all this. We are joined by love, Maureen. Will you remember that? Because it will always be so. Remember, please, for all time, that I love you, dearest child...

MAUREEN (*moved by her father's sincerity*) Yes, Dad.

MASKELL Time to go. You lead the way.

She turns her back on him, leads the way out of the room.

36   The stairway

Maureen comes nervously down the broken stairs. She looks back to her father following.

MASKELL Do not turn round, Maureen. Do not turn round...

37   The cottage back garden

The camera shows us Jean behind the low wall and pans round to give her point of view. The rear door of the cottage opens and Maureen comes slowly out. She gets fifteen feet out into the overgrown garden and turns. We all hear the sound of a shot gun from inside the cottage. The birds in the garden and in the trees rise up in fear.

MAUREEN (*screams*) No Dad.

Maskell staggers out of rear door of cottage. He walks through a half collapsed cold frame, smashing glass with his feet as he stumbles forward.

The camera cuts to Jean as she gets to her feet. As we hear Maureen's scream, we focus on Jean, full of disbelief and anger at herself, for what's happened.

JEAN Oh God, no...

We cut to a ground-level shot of the feet and half the laid-out body of Maskell.

Jean and some others come up, look down. We can see little sideways

*critical looks to her from these males – she was in charge, this should not
have happened.*

*The camera leaves her to track with Sergeant Beck round to the front of
the cottage. Beck intercepts the firearms officers, but is joined by the journalist.*

JOURNALIST Have you a statement, Sergeant Beck?

BECK (*stopping and pondering*) I have, Mr Cowley. It rained a little
this morning. Then it was fine. (*looks up*) Now it'll be raining again shortly. Don't quote me till you clear it with our
PR bloke at HQ. Right?

JOURNALIST (*flat*) Thanks.

*In the background we see sub-divisional Superintendent Lake's private
Triumph 2000 pull in beside the ambulance. He gets out, goes over to see
the ambulance men putting the corpse into ambulance. In longshot he has
a few words with the doctor, then turns, sees Jean heading up to and
getting into her Escort, and just sitting there. He leaves the doctor, and
crosses to her. The car window's down.*

LAKE How the hell did this happen? Weren't you able to make
any dialogue at all with him?

JEAN We simply didn't have time to develop a dialogue.

LAKE Let's talk about you, not "we". Didn't you attempt to
negotiate any deal with him? What went wrong?

JEAN You can see what went wrong, sir.

*We focus on Jean, a little note of defiance in her voice. It's the sort of
incident that's resulted, at this moment, in her feeling so put down she
might resign or ask for a transfer to Juvenile Bureau or Community
Liaison.*

LAKE Well, it's a helluva cock up, isn't it?

JEAN Yes, sir.

LAKE I'll go to Headquarters, try to start to explain this. You'd
better get down to your report.

JEAN I have to clear up here, sir.

LAKE No. Chief Inspector Morell is coming. He d better take
charge.

He turns and goes. Beck comes over to her.

BECK (*thumbs towards ambulance*) City or County morgue, boss?

JEAN City. Organise Mrs Maskell to identify the body, then wait
here for Chief Inspector Morell. After that, pick up Mr
Porter, I'm going to find that daughter of his, and that
bloke, "Peter".

BECK Yes, boss.

Beck starts to go off.

Jean suddenly angry.

JEAN Sergeant Beck!

BECK (*turning*) Yes, boss?

JEAN (*getting out of her car*) Come here, Sergeant Beck.

JEAN Don't you ever call me "Boss" again. Call me "Ma'am". Don't ever open a car door for me, or an office door. I can do that myself. Don't ever put your hand out to help me climb over anything. Is that clear?

BECK Yes, ma'am.

JEAN I'm here to stay, Joseph. So forget all those jokes about women, and your snide looks. Then we'll be all right, you and me. Clear?

BECK Yes, ma'am.

Jean gets back into the car, starts it, and drives off. The camera zooms in on Beck's reaction: thoughtful, not angry. It's as if he's been waiting for her to sort it out between the two of them. She now has. And he'll go along with it.

38 Jean's office. Hartley Police Station (evening)

The desk light on. Jean has just finished writing the report. She reaches for her phone, dials.

JEAN (*into phone*) Tom.

39 A corner of the Darblays' kitchen

We see Tom holding the phone with an oven glove.

TOM Hello, sweetheart.

40 Jean's office

Intercutting: Tom and Jean

JEAN How did the interview go?

TOM Not bad. Say they'll let me know. I'll tell you all about it. Come home.

JEAN I'm just putting a report in for the clerk to type. I'll have to come back later tonight to sign and dispatch it.

TOM I've cooked a bloody capon, it'll spoil if you don't come home soon.

JEAN Thanks, love.

For a moment she looks on the point of tears, as if she feels she's also let Tom down.

TOM What sort of day have you had?

JEAN Oh, not too good. I'm coming home now, love.

TOM Right. I'll put the kettle on.

JEAN Thanks, love.

Coins

Ray Jenkins

The Cast

Inspector Jean Darblay

Sergeant Joseph Beck

PC Roland Bentley

WPC Gilbert

Tom Darblay

Carol

Kenny

Major Adams

Kay Brown

Bob Nicholas

Pat Nicholas

Councillor Blake

Two PCs from the neighbouring force of Turley

Coins

1 A Shelter (night)

The episode opens inside a shelter. There is total darkness except for a powerful torch, wonderingly picking out provision-stacked shelving. The light settles on a row of heavily packed plastic bags.

KENNY (*whispering*) What do you think?

CAROL (*whispering*) Don't know.

A match is struck.

CAROL Y'could burn it!

KENNY Sh! It's plastic, it won't spread, daft!

Sure enough; the flame is held against the packet and a hole burns. The match is dropped and the contents tasted.

KENNY Flour-power!

They both giggle, companionably, then move on. We take in more and more packed shelving. Then the light reaches a pile of blankets, the beam is held on the girl's face. She is fourteen, blonde, her face clumsily made up with mascara and powder.

KENNY Shall we?

There is a slight pause, then she nods, giving a big grin.

KENNY Take hold then.

She takes the torch and the boy quickly removes two heavy-duty grey blankets.

KENNY How many do you reckon we need?

CAROL Four. Two each.

KENNY Right.

Another two are removed and the gap in the goods is obvious. The torch searches the floor. In the corner is a camp bed. The torch steadies.

KENNY Y'have to promise – no fighting ever with us?

The beam picks up her face. She is serious staring beyond the torch.

2 Adams's House (morning)

The camera shows us the house on a ridge overlooking the chimneys and

back-to-backs. We can see PC Bentley's bike leaning against the hedge outside the house.
The back kitchen door opens and Major Adams, sixty-three, emerges, followed by Bentley.
Adams is stocky, a store-sergeant who rose to be an officer. He makes no attempt to hide his roots; his bearing is still military.
He gives a large torch to Bentley and keeps one himself.
ADAMS Here, lad, you'll be needing it.
BENTLEY Thank you, sir.
ADAMS Mind the rosebeds.
They both make their way past the rosebeds towards a large shelter. They descend steps to it and Adams indicates the lock. He unlocks it.
BENTLEY How did they get in?
ADAMS On a shaft of bloody moonlight – they must've picked this.
The door opens – well-oiled ... into darkness.

3   Inside the shelter

BENTLEY Aren't there any lights?
ADAMS (*indicating with a torch*) They took the key to the generator.
BENTLEY (*turning on his torch*) Why would they do that, Major?
ADAMS You're the bloody detective.
BENTLEY No, not for a couple of weeks yet, sir, I'm only a constable –
ADAMS (*heavy*) So I couldn't put the light on to see what they've done.
Bentley's torch goes over the neat rows of tins (some with quite old labels). He can't help smiling – it's an Aladdin's cave.
BENTLEY What've you got all this down here for?
ADAMS I was in the war. The next one won't be fought with guns.
BENTLEY I've never seen half these labels.
He focuses on tins of bully beef.
BENTLEY How many minutes do they give you nowadays before you put your head in a paper bag?
ADAMS I'm not mad. But when Roos-ia does come, I'll have everything here necessary – I won't be caught.
BENTLEY You're not going to *eat* them are you?
ADAMS They won't blow – down here's a constant temperature – look, two's missing –

BENTLEY (*replacing a tin*) Tell you what – heave a load of this over to the station – we'll help you shift it.

ADAMS (*of other gaps*) In addition, they've taken two sets of knives and forks.

Elsewhere.

ADAMS Primus stove.

Elsewhere.

ADAMS Three tins of pork sausages, two corned beef – two blankets and the generator key.

BENTLEY (*serious*) So you reckon they'll be back, do you? The key, I mean?

ADAMS (*heavy*) No doubt they didn't count on me inspecting the place daily. So when you come back with a live detective you can show 'em this –

The punctured bags. Bentley can't resist tasting it. Then he is shown the floor.

ADAMS Spent matches.

Then the bed.

ADAMS And that. Exactly as I found it.

Bentley crosses to it. Two blankets are rumpled. He picks up the edge of one of them, then sniffs it.

BENTLEY Make-up.

ADAMS (*still*) My privacy's been invaded.

4   The desk area of Hartley Police Station

Sergeant Beck reads over Bentley's shoulder as he writes up his report.

BECK (*pointing*) Two "s's" in "necessary".

BENTLEY (*mock-straight*) I reckon it's clear as mud – a group of travelling players who fry cornbeef and flour patties over a primus stove, then wrap themselves up in blankets and play hunt the key. Or kids.

BECK Happen.

BENTLEY (*altering the word carefully*) Have you ever thought: freeze time, like now – and two girls – one's on the way to being Wonder Woman – or Inspector –

Beck sees Jean, who has entered unnoticed, and steps back.

BENTLEY And another's already put her first toe into a life of crime –

JEAN Which one are you dealing with?

Bentley whirls to attention, clumsily, and embarrassed: Beck only just controls a grin: Jean crosses to the desk and reads his report.

JEAN Well?

BENTLEY He's got *everything* in case of nuclear attack – there's labels in there nobody's seen! He's bananas.

JEAN It's still a break-in.

Pause.

BENTLEY Yes, ma'am.

JEAN This list of items missing – what does it suggest to you? Gypsies? Tramps? Kids? – leaving out the local Rep on the rampage? Well?

BENTLEY There's a female there – make-up powder on the bed.

BECK You're too young to know about face powder!

JEAN Did you bring it in so that we could check?

BENTLEY No, ma'am.

JEAN You mention matches – did you bring them in for forensic?

BENTLEY No, ma'am.

JEAN Do so in future. For the moment – it's your beat – have you checked with people either side?

No reply.

JEAN So – what do you do?

BENTLEY Go back, ma'am and –

JEAN Right. You check his place twice a night – and make sure you do because I might be cruising round the area.

She goes.

BECK You've done well, son – (*winks*) Just like being home, isn't it – telling off by the missus – "get the dishes done", "mend the cat" –

BENTLEY (*sore*) She's only rattled because it's face-powder. I *know* it's a woman – I'll get her!

BECK (*tapping phone*) In the meantime – ring the old boy. Tell him to keep an eye out. If it was that easy they'll come again – and if they do he's to ring here – (*he smiles*) and I'll get your face round there fast as Concorde. Move!

5 A section of the Darblays' lounge – looking through to kitchen (night)

The room is in darkness except for light from the kitchen area.
In silhouette, Jean, in uniform, is framed in the doorway. She takes one step into the lounge.

JEAN (*whisper*) Tom?
No reply.
JEAN Tom?
A rustle from the sofa.
TOM (*sleepy*) Uh... Yes... Hello.
JEAN You sound all in.
TOM (*rousing himself slightly*) I've been traipsing around with
everybody all day long asking questions. I think my feet are
still out the back moaning. Design was all answers. Social
work's all asking questions.
JEAN Do you know what my nickname is?
Silence.
TOM (*sleepily*) Wonder Woman.
JEAN How did you know?
TOM What time is it?
JEAN Cuppa?

6 Adams's house (night)

*The garden gate clicks open. A figure gangles into deep foreground, paus-
ing as it scans the house for signs of life.*
Nothing.
*Stealthily it creeps up the pathway leading past the house towards the
underground shelter. We recognise the shape of Bentley.*
*Suddenly Bentley stumbles. A cacophony of rattling cans and bells and
then he is nowhere to be seen. Almost immediately the back door bursts
open, and another figure (Adams) rushes out, garden fork in hand.*
*We find Bentley, distinctly the worse for wear, slumped in the bearpit
surrounded by brushwood and briar. He peers up to see Adams, a dark
shape against the background of the house, peering into the pit.*
Adams snorts in disgust.

7 Jean's office (morning)

*Bentley stands, one hand with an Elastoplast dressing, a scratch showing
on his cheek, terrified, before Jean's desk. Between them his torn, filthy
uniform jacket.*
Jean is reading from a report.
JEAN ...whilst walking down the path at the rear of the house,

I fell over some debris – 'is' not 'es' – caught my uniform in some shrubbery, causing a number of tears to the material".

She throws down the report in (mock) disgust and stares at Bentley.

JEAN Policemen don't fall over.

BENTLEY It was dark, ma'am!

JEAN Even in the dark.

BENTLEY No, ma'am.

JEAN I've pointed out the error of his ways to Major Adams and tonight when you patrol again, the tripwires – any form of trap – will not be there.

Bentley nods as the telephone rings, but she lets it ring and stands as she concludes.

JEAN We'll leave the report stand, shall we, to save you any embarrassment at Headquarters?

Bentley goes swiftly as she picks up the telephone.

JEAN Inspector Darblay.

Then Bentley turns at the door, having realised he's left the coat, to find her holding it out to him with her free hand – he grabs it and goes – slamming the door.

Jean winces.

JEAN (*hard*) That has been covered – I'll take two off the late shift, one off night duty for the prisoners' van and if we sense any further trouble we'll keep the early shift on.

8 Inside the shelter (night)

In total silence, efficiently, Carol is removing yet more tinned food from the shelves and carefully packing them into an ex-army webbing pack hanging round her neck in front of her. With very, very precise movements she places the tins in the bag without a sound, one-handed, the other holding a torch. She is concentrating as she places the last one into the bag – then as her free hand reaches out and takes the last tin, she is grabbed fiercely from behind by Major Adams. She struggles with the ferocity of an alley cat. And what we can see of what happens is from the wildly waving torch of Carol. His own shines directly into her face. Then unexpectedly, he in turn is jumped on from behind by Kenny. They struggle wordlessly, then as the boy's weight swings the older man round and therefore off-balance, Carol uses the opportunity to ram the edge of the tin she is holding down onto the back of his hand. He shrieks with pain and releases her, falling back against the shelving.

KENNY Let's get out!!

And we hear him clatter up the steps. But there is a pause…

KENNY C'mon!

…while Carol obviously worries about having hurt an old man – which allows him to shine his torch full at her. We see that she is in anorak and jeans. Then she turns and bolts away, up the steps, and slams the door behind her.

As quickly as he can, the Major struggles to the door, pulls it open … on to darkness.

9   The desk area at the police station (night)

BECK (*at radio control*) Hartley here. To all units. Wanted in con-
nection with offence of burglary at 29 Havering Road,
female, thirteen–fifteen years, height five foot two inches,
blonde, wearing green anorak and jeans. 7189 Bentley to
investigate at scene. Inspector Darblay on her way there.
Acknowledge please. Over.

Jean comes through from her office – putting on her hat on her way out.

BENTLEY (*distorted*) 7189. Message received, Sarge. On my way.
Out.

10   Inside the shelter (night)

Now the shelter is brightly lit, and we can take in the full extent of the major's provisions, etc.

In fact, with one hand bandaged, he is making a note, on paper, of all that has been taken. At one point his hand is near Bentley's Elastoplas-tered hand.

BENTLEY Snap!

He grins at the old man who does not grin back.

ADAMS Where was the tea-lad when it mattered?

JEAN He's been here twice.

Jean is examining the place minutely for clues.

ADAMS I pay rates, woman!

JEAN (*after a tiny freeze*) 'Inspector', Major. He's got a big patch,
he can't stay just *here* all the time!

ADAMS If I'd left my traps up I'd've got them!

JEAN They came in from the road?

ADAMS I'd've put more! All over the place.

JEAN When you saw them first – you should've rung us then!

ADAMS Happen, but you hear this – officer or not – those traps go back!

JEAN I'd rather you let us run things, Major – it's dangerous taking the law into your own hands –

ADAMS Don't lecture me!

JEAN – for others and yourself!

ADAMS I can look after myself.

JEAN How's your hand?

There is a pause.

ADAMS Back in my kitchen, you take a damned good look at the plates on my dresser, Inspector, because, Inspector, you'll find every one, spotless, unscarred, never a crack, and, if the Holy Ghost walked in, it could eat off any one it chose. Only one gets used at a time. Because I eat on my own, drink solo, nobody digs my garden – *I* do it – I know every bloody crocus by name. I can manage. Always have. You know why, Inspector?

JEAN No.

ADAMS So you don't know everything. Pity eh? Well, if I'm asked a question, and I don't know the answer, I make an excuse, leave the room and go to the bog – where I keep a book of answers – me.

Jean smiles.

ADAMS Good eh?

JEAN You're very lucky.

ADAMS Oh no.

He takes down a bar of chocolate and stares at it.

ADAMS Once upon a bloody time I was a lad. Then I had mates. Then one by one, details consisting of *their* mates went out into the sand and buried them. (*tapping his chest*) 'Q' Adams. When you've handed out every bit of webbing, every item of clothing, blankets and boots to a whole Regiment and if you want to get them back you have to pick them off tank-metal, you end up not liking what people do to people. You follow?

JEAN I think so.

He breaks chocolate for Bentley and Jean; they take it.

ADAMS And you end up not wanting to know. Eat it. You won't die.

JEAN (*softly*) Well...we *do* want to know.

ADAMS I suppose you're doing your job.

JEAN (*slowly*) You...got a good look at the girl?

(*He nods*).

JEAN Do you know her?

ADAMS (*finally*) No, but...

Jean waits.

ADAMS She reminds me of the lass who used to do the paper-
round – a year back. Mind you I'm not sure.

JEAN One minute man-traps the next –

ADAMS They grow up so quick. That's all I'm saying.

JEAN Do you know her name?

ADAMS No.

JEAN Do you still get your papers delivered from the same place?

ADAMS Roberts'.

JEAN Down Ainsley Road.

He nods. Jean turns on Bentley who swallows his chocolate lumpily.

JEAN Get on to Control, tell him to give the description to the
tobacconists, ask them if they know such a girl and what's
her name and address.

BENTLEY It's quarter past eleven –

JEAN I know the time. Key-holders card. The tobacconists'll be
on the phone –

BENTLEY Yes, ma'am –

JEAN (*hard*) We've got a girl – and her friend – out at this time
of night. If they didn't get what they were after they'll try
elsewhere and we'll have another call!

Bentley goes, unclipping his radio.

Adams hands Jean his list.

ADAMS There's your list, minus the chocolate.

11 Outside a large Victorian house (morning)

*Bentley, driving, draws up before a large, square Victorian house that,
even before we enter it, has the air of a local authority Home, rambling
over three storeys.*

JEAN You stay here.

BENTLEY Ma'am.

*Before he can be polite, Jean is out and hurrying up the steps and dis-
appearing inside. Bentley takes out chewing-gum and stares unenthusiast-
ically out at the world.*

12   The Warden's office

Kay Brown, an easy-going woman of fifty, in kaftan and pink eye-patch, rises enthusiastically.

KAY Jean! Come in, come in.

JEAN Kay.

KAY Business or business?

JEAN Business.

KAY Damn – I fancied a sherry.

She has cleared a chair of laundered sheets. They are old friends.

JEAN I want to see Carol Bampton.

Kay looks, surprised.

JEAN She's here, isn't she?

KAY (*nods*) Half-term. Is it news about her mother?

JEAN (*thrown*) No.

KAY She can't be in trouble.

JEAN Kay, listen. We have reason to believe on two occasions she's burgled a house –

KAY When!

JEAN Two out of three of the last evenings.

KAY What time?

JEAN Around midnight.

KAY Jean – the fact that I look like Captain Hook lately doesn't mean either I'm a sadist *or* careless. She's been here – there are rules in a place like this!

JEAN Is there a care-order for her? – because there isn't on my records.

KAY Of course there isn't. She's only here because her mother's in the County General – and not likely to come out. A stroke.

JEAN Has she any other relatives?

KAY None. She helps with the little ones. Then like all of us she's locked up at nights!

JEAN Have you had *any* trouble with her?

KAY Obviously she's finding it difficult adjusting – this isn't home, it's *a* Home. She's not over fond of lights out and telly off. I admit she tends to blame everybody but circumstances for her mother's condition – but does that make her a thief?

Kay is beginning to regret her hasty, initial, defence.

JEAN We think two are involved. Has she a friend – ?

KAY N–no. She'll only talk with the little ones – it's where she is now.

JEAN Boy-friends?

KAY (*after shaking her head doubtfully*) But...after all my...control over her is necessarily loose – she's not here "officially" if you see what I mean...hm.

JEAN What does *that* mean?

KAY Pauline does the meal supervision – it's the only time I get to myself – she did say – the last week or two – Carol didn't eat everything – anything wrapped or fruit she takes out. Just observation.

JEAN I think I'd better see her now.

KAY (*dialling two numbers with a wry expression*) You prove I'm slipping and that's the last time you're drinking here.

(*into phone*) Ann, can you spare Carol for a few minutes, love ...yes, my office, thanks. (*telephone down*) What's she supposed to have taken?

13 The lower landing of the Home

Leaving the sounds of small ones playing above her, Carol skips down onto the landing – where there is a large sash-window looking down onto the street. As she passes to descend yet again, she does a double-take and tiptoes back to look down. We see her point of view: the police car is obvious, as too is PC Bentley, who suddenly reaches for his personal radio. Carol dodges back in panic. Then she dashes back along a corridor joining the landing. The camera precedes her into her room. It is simple – with a bed, wardrobe, tiny table and brightly covered curtains over a barred window. Carol enters, grabs her anorak and a neck purse and hurries out.

14 Outside the Home

The camera cuts to the police car.

Bentley is on his personal radio.

BECK (*distorted*) He's here at the desk, demanding to see the Inspector – (*less volume*) get her if you can or there'll be blood on the walls.

BENTLEY I'll tell her now, sarge. Out.

He puts down his P/R and smartly leaves the car and runs up the steps and into the Home.

15 The hallway of the Home

As he enters at a burst he is pulled up short by the sight of Carol on the stairs.
He recognises the blonde hair, green anorak and jeans, and she panics at the sight of him and realises his recognition. There is a fractional pause. Then she dashes down the remaining stairs and makes for the kitchen area beyond. Bentley sets off in pursuit. We can hear angry noises in the kitchen.

16 The rear garden of the Home

The small garden is part grass with a climbing frame and part rubbish – i.e. charitable but useless donations to the home – toys, baths, chairs. At top speed Carol bursts from the kitchen; skilfully threads her way through the rubbish then up onto a shed as Bentley appears.
BENTLEY Come on, love, get down. You'll fall!
Carol ignores him, runs the length of the shed to where there is a pressed gap in what seems like barbed wire "protecting" the home. She carefully straddles the wall and drops to the other side – something, one feels, she's done many times before. Bentley, slower and with more circumspection, does the same, eventually.
As Bentley drops into the street, seventy yards down the road, he sees the green anorak turn inside a side street. Bentley runs, with all the indignity a uniform and speed confers. People watch. An old lady, as he passes, even tries to clobber him with her stick.
BENTLEY (*alarmed*) Leave off!!
And he reaches the turning.
It is a dead end. No sign of the girl. She could not have scaled the walls because they are high, brick sides of mills or factories. He walks forward cautiously – Carol has flattened herself against the side of a small niche. She doesn't move as he breathlessly approaches to within a couple of yards of her.
BENTLEY Carol?
He moves in again and stops. Now we and he can see Carol's eyes – rimmed with defiant tears.
BENTLEY Carol?
She hasn't moved a millimetre – her palms pressing into the brick.
BENTLEY C'mon, luv.
CAROL (*steady*) I'm not.
BENTLEY You're not what?
CAROL Your love.

Bentley reaches out to take her shoulder but slowly Carol turns her face to the corner of the wall and stands there, noiselessly, like a reprimanded child in class.

17 The Warden's office

Kay and Bentley are standing: Jean and Carol are seated facing each other across the Warden's desk.

JEAN My name's Inspector Darblay. I think you know what I've come about?

CAROL No. (*She looks peevishly at the floor.*)

JEAN Why did you run away?

CAROL Don't like the police.

JEAN People who don't usually have a reason – what's yours?

CAROL You're picking on us.

JEAN "Us"?

CAROL Teenagers.

JEAN When were you picked on?

KAY Carol.

CAROL Not me, friends.

JEAN Boy friends?

No reply.

JEAN You've got one, haven't you?

No reply.

JEAN Aren't you proud of him?

CAROL None of your business.

KAY No need to be rude.

Silence. Jean tries a new tack.

JEAN We seem to have got off on the wrong foot...

No reply.

JEAN Mrs Brown has told me about why you're here. I'm sorry about your mother.

Silence: another new tack.

JEAN All right. Three nights ago you went into a shelter attached to number 29 Havering Road and took away tinned food, a primus stove, blankets and cutlery. Where are they now?

Silence.

JEAN You did, didn't you?

Silence.

BENTLEY You use make-up?

Annoyed, Jean motions him to shut up.

CAROL (*defiant*) I'm old enough!
Bentley is pleased with himself.
JEAN And again, last night – only this time a Major Adams caught you – but you got away. (*Silence*) Why don't you answer me?
CAROL Because I was here. I was in here at eleven o'clock.
JEAN I haven't mentioned any time. Why did you say eleven?
CAROL You can ask anybody here! You find out.
JEAN I intend to. Mrs Brown, do you have any objection to me looking in this young lady's room.
Carol breaks for the first time.
CAROL It's private!
JEAN & KAY (*together*) So's the Major's shelter.
    Carol, if you've got nothing to hide, you can't mind, can you, love?
The girl looks in pure hatred towards Bentley.

18 Carol's room

Jean is already searching the wardrobe expertly, while Bentley is on his knees raking under the bed. Kay, at the door, worried, watches Carol who stands at the barred window, trying to appear indifferent to the search. Jean shows two or three wafer bars of chocolate hidden amongst clothes to Kay who nods miserably. Jean turns to see Carol watching Bentley who, in the act of levering himself up from the floor, pushes off the pillow. Carol winces, then looks quickly out of the window.
BENTLEY (*upright*) Nothing, ma'am.
CAROL I told you.
Jean crosses to the pillow, lifts it, and picks up four photos in a strip, obviously taken in a station booth. Three of the photos are of Kenny, one of them has the two kids together.
JEAN Who's this?
CAROL Leave him alone!
JEAN He's nice. Your boy-friend?
Carol, one feels, wants to snatch the photos away, but doesn't move.
CAROL Keep him out of it! He hasn't done anything!
JEAN You did it. On your own?
CAROL Yes!
JEAN You went down that shelter on your own? In the dark?
CAROL (*lying*) Yes!!

JEAN Two blankets and all the rest are pretty bulky – you couldn't carry all that out on your own.

CAROL I did.

JEAN All right, where is it all now?

CAROL Sold them!

JEAN Where?

CAROL I threw them all away. Give me them pictures.

JEAN You've just told me you sold them –

CAROL Well I'm just telling you I chucked them away! Give me them pictures.

KAY Carol!

JEAN (*deliberate*) No, Kay – leave it.

She looks at the photos. We get a close up view too.

The face of Kenny is impish, thin, and apparently devoid of malice.

JEAN Carol – are you on the pill?

CAROL I know what you're saying – it's not that.

JEAN Then why?

CAROL He makes me laugh. All the time.

JEAN What's his name? (*No reply.*) Then we'll have to go round the schools, shops –

CAROL You're not going to show my pictures – they're mine! You won't find him!

It is Jean versus Carol.

CAROL Am I going to be arrested?

JEAN For the moment you'll be reported. A summons *might* be issued and you'd have to go to Juvenile Court eventually.

CAROL I can still stay here?

JEAN (*nodding*) But under much stricter supervision.

CAROL You going to tell mum about this?

JEAN If it's going to be harmful to her, no.

CAROL If you don't tell her, I'll tell his name. But not where he is. I'll never do that.

JEAN No promises, Carol.

CAROL He's...Kenny. That's all.

Jean carefully tears one snap from the top of the strip and hands back the others. Jean nods to Bentley who smartly opens the door.

JEAN Are you good with locks. (*No reply.*) All the blankets and things – they're with him? He's camping?

CAROL I'm not telling.

JEAN (*going*) Thank you, Mrs Brown.

As Jean reaches the landing window, she turns to Bentley.

JEAN If you see that lass in the street, wandering or with a boy, or within a mile of Havering Road – bring her to me, not here!

BENTLEY Yes, ma'am.

19 Carol's room

Carol is at the barred window.

KAY You don't run away, Carol. If you do you leave her no alternative but Court...and maybe a secure unit. You're not being let off. You've committed a crime.

CAROL (*zombie-like*) What's that?

KAY Burglary.

CAROL It's first time. I'll only be cautioned.

KAY Not always.

CAROL They won't find him because he isn't there.

20 The desk area of the police station

As Jean and Bentley enter, a burly man of thirty-eight, looking like a truck driver, gets up from the seat in the corner.

BLAKE Inspector – I've been waiting here forty-five minutes!

Beck tries to warn her, but too late. She turns.

JEAN Ah! Councillor!

BLAKE I've got a job as well.

JEAN (*to Beck*) Why wasn't I told the Coun –

BLAKE You were! (*pointing*) I saw it being sent out on the radio!

Bentley steps forward.

BENTLEY That was the message I was coming in to tell you when I saw the girl, ma'am.

Jean contemplates homicide.

BENTLEY I'm sorry. I forgot.

JEAN (*smoothly*) A breakdown in communication, I apologise, Councillor. Sergeant would you mind getting two coffees.

BLAKE Forget that – you listen to me! I've got the list of off-street parking for the supporters coaches. I'm telling you they're not going down Castle Street or Verney Street. You remember year before last – pissing in the hedges, abuse, broken milk bottles – even a gate pinched. You change t'venue or I'm telling you I'm off to the Police Committee – happen they'll be listening! I'm speaking for those residents – it's my ward, cup-tie or no – they've even told me they'll barricade both ends.

JEAN Can you spare me *one* minute?

As he stops she puts the photo down in front of Beck and continues rapidly.

JEAN Get a message to all units next time in the station and before going off duty look at this photograph. I want an address for the lad in it – he's called Kenny. And he may be camping out.

BECK (*impressed*) Yes, ma'am.

JEAN Get WPC Gilbert from Juvenile Liaison up here. Let her see it. Tell her to collect a copy and go round Ridgefield Comprehensive and St Josephs. Check with Northern CRO re absconders from detention centres and borstals – he's obviously on the trot from somewhere. (*As Beck moves to comply she turns to a slightly abashed Blake.*) Now, Councillor – football!

21 Mrs Nicholas's House (afternoon)

The house is in a more attractive rural area than Hartley, at the end of a row, detached, with a garden at the back. A Mini-Traveller sweeps confidently off the road, down the side of the house and comes to a stop before the side garage doors. Mrs Pat Nicholas, thirty-five, steps out, trim and reasonably well-dressed. She reaches on a hidden ledge for the key. When the doors swing open Kenny Nicholas, a tiny fourteen-year-old, as trim and alert as his mother, grins and holds out the key.

KENNY Hello, mum.

Pat, after her first surprise, isn't angry. She just grins down at her son, both grins identical.

PAT Y'little devil!

22 Jean's office (afternoon)

Jean, elbows on street-maps and a pad before her with street names listed and some crossed out. She listens to WPC Gilbert, twenty-one, who is in plain clothes, and holds a copy of Kenny's photo.

GILBERT I think I know this boy –

JEAN Then why don't I –

45

GILBERT Oh no, ma'am, it wasn't a crime or a traffic case.

JEAN Ah!

GILBERT He was at the Juvenile Court – oh, six months back I think it was truancy – the local authority dealt with it.

JEAN What's his name?

GILBERT I forget – but I'll go and ring the clerk's office at the court. They'll have it. If I remember right somebody told me the mother had to be removed from the hearing – she slung her bag at the father.

JEAN (*pointing to the phone*) Use that.

23   Kenny's room at his father's house (afternoon)

The room is small but totally chaotic. The mess of a teenager with imag- ination but limited finance.

BECK (*off vision*) Can we see the room?

NICHOLAS (*off vision*) I'll get in more trouble with the court!

The door is pushed open by a small man, Bob Nicholas, thirty-six, but looking older. A night-worker, he has been roused from his afternoon sleep, so looks at his worst. He holds the door back for Sergeant Beck and WPC Gilbert to edge their way in.

BECK Forget the Court – what about your lad!

NICHOLAS (*to Gilbert*) What about him!

BECK You know where he is?

NICHOLAS (*lamely*) It's half-term.

Beck has no idea where to start in the mess.

BECK You on pre-payment meters?

NICHOLAS He wouldn't steal!

BECK Are you!

NICHOLAS Y – yes.

BECK Go and check 'em will you!

Nicholas nods and goes.

GILBERT Steve McQueen come back, all is forgiven.

Beck opens an old wardrobe door, very few clothes hang there.

BECK Didn't see an outside coat downstairs did you?

GILBERT No, sarge.

Both rummage, Gilbert examines a pinboard full of soccer photos.

GILBERT Well, he's got taste.

NICHOLAS (*downstairs*) Hey!

BECK What?

NICHOLAS Meters're alright but m'candles've gone!

BECK Candles? Come up here Mr Nicholas (*lowering his voice*) before I stick one up your nose.

They rummage. Nicholas enters, out of breath, strapping on his watch.

NICHOLAS I keep 'em for power cuts.

BECK When did you last see Kenny?

NICHOLAS (*looking at his watch*) Couple of days?

BECK I'm asking you.

NICHOLAS Couple of days.

BECK He *lives* here doesn't he?

NICHOLAS I work night down Pattersons, so I sleep in the day. (*aggressively*) You have to take the best money where you can nowadays. So I see him tea-time.

GILBERT When does he eat?

NICHOLAS There's money in the jar for the chippy – then I cook properly at weekends. Or takeaway.

BECK Mr Nicholas? I want you to have a good look round this paradise and tell me what's missing. Will you do that?

NICHOLAS Yes.

He does so.

BECK Has he got a Post Office Savings book?

NICHOLAS No. I give him money.

BECK A bike?

NICHOLAS No. I can't see anything that's gone. It's all rumpled.

Beck's look withers.

BECK Keep looking.

NICHOLAS Why're you asking me all this?

BECK We think he's gone.

NICHOLAS Where?

BECK That's what you're helping us find out.

They watch him unitl he's aware they're staring at him: so he stops.

NICHOLAS I can't find anything.

GILBERT Where do you think he'd go, Mr Nicholas?

Nicholas winces.

GILBERT Your wife's?

NICHOLAS (*fiercely*) I told him never to!

BECK But he *might* go there? (*no reply.*) What's the address? (*no reply*) He's your *son*, Mr Nicholas!

NICHOLAS He wouldn't go there, no!

He suddenly whirls and makes for a tiny desk and empties the second drawer.

Then the top drawer, obviously what he's expected to find there isn't.

Nicholas sits on the bed.

BECK (*gentler*) Something wrong?

NICHOLAS Coins.

Pause.

BECK What's that?

GILBERT Coins?

NICHOLAS You're right. He has gone. He wouldn't go anywhere without them. See I...

He stares at the empty drawers.

NICHOLAS When I give him money...he buys old coins. He can sit here hours – just turning 'em over. He knows every prime minister since Walpole.

He looks at them, upset.

NICHOLAS 1760 or thereabouts.

A long unhappy silence.

NICHOLAS Yeah, he's gone to her.

He draws his fingers down over his eyes.

NICHOLAS She's...with a singer. He does the clubs.

BECK Where's that?

NICHOLAS Clubs?

BECK The singer.

NICHOLAS She never bothered dressing up when she was here. No conversation – just LP's all the time. She says she does for him. I bet she does. Housekeeper! Hah!

He looks directly at Gilbert.

NICHOLAS It might be rumpled here – but you notice it's clean? That's me – not her! That court was right – suggesting he lived here – not with her!

Gilbert nods.

NICHOLAS They're little trays. In black velvet.

Silence.

BECK What's the address.

NICHOLAS 47...Aleby Close, Turley.

BECK That's thirty miles. How do you reckon he's got there?

Nicholas shrugs.

BECK You been there?

NICHOLAS I tried to get her back.

BECK (*finally*) O.K., Mr Nicholas, thanks. We'll do our best.

They turn to go.

NICHOLAS Do you think I ought to go to work tonight?

BECK (*no longer angry, and showing pity*) He's your son. If he was mine I'd be out looking.

NICHOLAS Somebody's got to earn money. They all need it.

24 The desk area of the police station (afternoon)

Jean enters and goes straight to Beck, who shows her a slip of paper.

BECK That's the address, ma'am – but it's out of our patch.

JEAN I'll get the locals to call round and search. In the meantime get him circulated as a missing person and wanted for interview suspected buglary and make sure his particulars are on the National Computer.

She looks at her watch.

JEAN In...five minutes I want to go and have another look at Castle Street and Verney Street.

Beck nods: Bentley comes in.

BENTLEY The schools've closed, ma'am.

JEAN I think we know where he is –

She goes.

BENTLEY Where's that, sarge?

BECK San Francisco.

25 The Warden's office in the Home (afternoon)

Kay is working at her desk.

KAY Come in.

Carol enters, shyly, already in her anorak, eyes made up.

KAY Hello.

CAROL I-I finished with the little ones and I've had tea. I–I want to go and see mum.

Kay tries to work out whether this is a con or not.

CAROL Visitin's five to eight.

KAY I know. How are you going to get there?

CAROL Bus and walk back.

KAY I've got a better idea – I'll take you.

Disappointment flickers over Carol's face for a second.

CAROL You can trust me, I'll be back by seven.

KAY No bother. What're you going to take her?

CAROL Chocolate.

26 Mrs Nicholas's hallway (late afternoon)

A police constable in uniform stands in a position from which he has glimpses of the kitchen and the lounge. A second police constable finishes in the lounge and makes for the stairs. At the top he reaches up and taps the trapdoor to the loft. It doesn't give. Mrs Nicholas, furious, watches from below, arms folded.

27   Outside the hospital (early evening)

Kay's car stops in the roadway and Carol gets out, waves, and makes for the reception – and disappears inside. Kay puts the car into gear – and waits.
Carol emerges from a side entrance and from her point of view we see Kay's car drive off.
Carol reverses her anorak and runs hard for the factory part of the town, her face eager.

28   Mrs Nicholas's hallway (early evening)

With a last glance back towards the bedroom the second police constable follows Pat downstairs. She is grim-faced, her arms still folded tightly across her chest and she wordlessly walks straight past the first police constable and into her kitchen. The two policemen exchange glances as if to imply "What a dog!"

29   Outside the hospital (late evening)

Carol, with her anorak still inside out, emerges from the reception and makes for Kay's car – which now has a cot strapped to the roof. Carol is carrying a small flat parcel half-tucked in her anorak. She gets into the car, smiling brightly.
CAROL Thanks.
KAY Your coat's on wrong!
CAROL I'm always doing that. It's like having two. Can we get back?
KAY How's your mother?
CAROL No change. She dribbles all the time.
Carol looks so defeated Kay ruffles her hair fondly before switching on the engine.
KAY What's the parcel?
CAROL (*casually*) A book I took her before.

They set off. Carol looking everywhere except at Kay, clamping the parcel to her.

CAROL Sister said there was no point bringing her chocolate.

30   The Darblays' kitchen (night)

Tom, cold-steel chisel in hand is seen through a cloud of plaster. He is looking down at a heavily painted wood shelf which he has ripped away from the wall. Jacket off, relaxed, Jean appears at the doorway.

JEAN Ugh! What're you doing!

TOM Parachuting.

JEAN Good grief.

TOM They're ugly – filthy – at the wrong height and – (*He kicks a fallen shelf.*) useless.

JEAN It was the right height for me – *what are you doing*?

TOM Doing it myself. Starting from scratch.

JEAN And how am I supposed to cook and hand things –

TOM (a) We both cook – and (b) there'll be new ones!

Jean looks from the mess back to her husband.

JEAN Well, you're the expert.

TOM Then stand aside, Rudolph.

He moves her slightly out of the way as he stacks the shelf.

TOM (*of the place*) Look, love, design principles are the same whether it's Concorde, coil-winders or Ideal Kitchen – proper use of space, aptness of materials – the proper matching of function to effect, efficiency to style.

JEAN Your style or mine?

TOM Ours.

JEAN Thanks very much.

TOM What does that mean?

JEAN It means you mean "ours" means "yours".

TOM Again?

JEAN How do you know what *my* idea of a kitchen is? Men may design them, women *work* in them – we've never talked about it!

Because this is demonstrably true, Tom prepares to attack the second shelf. Jean suddenly leans against it with her hands.

JEAN Why are these going?

TOM They're open, wasting space – I thought fitted cupboards the whole length – but of course I'm an impractical man

She stays where she is.

JEAN And where's the cooker going?

TOM Over there to release space for a freezer.

JEAN I want an extractor above the cooker.

TOM You can have an extractor there – it's an outside wall, or it can go there.

JEAN Next to the door and furthest from the lounge – God help our legs!

TOM One minute you don't want smells – next you want cabbage-stink next to the lounge.

JEAN I never said that.

The phone rings.

TOM The phone.

JEAN Damn!

They stare at each other – she holding the shelf, he poised to attack it. The phone goes on ringing.

JEAN (*grinning*) If I answer it promise you won't start again?

TOM Till you get back – OK.

JEAN (*slowly releasing her hands*) OK.

He makes an immediate joking jab with his chisel.

JEAN You!

Tom mouths a kiss, slaps his chisel down and goes in search of a beer during Jean's search for the phone – which is under a cloth acting as a dustsheet for the pots and pans removed from the shelves.

JEAN Hello?

TURLEY POLICE CONSTABLE (*voice distorted*) Turley station here ma'am, re your request for a search, 47 Aleby Close. I apologise for ringing, ma'am, but your sergeant said you wanted to be…

JEAN Yes. What happened?

POLICE CONSTABLE (*voice distorted*) Negative, ma'am.

JEAN (*disappointed*) Hm. What did you think of Mrs Nicholas?

POLICE CONSTABLE (*voice distorted*) Yes, she didn't like us much. In fact she hardly said a word, ma'am.

JEAN Is she worried about the boy?

Tom kisses her.

POLICE CONSTABLE (*voice distorted*) Tell you the truth – not much, no. Or she didn't let on.

JEAN Did you tell her he is suspected of burglary?

POLICE CONSTABLE (*voice distorted*) No, we only said he was missing from home.

JEAN All the more reason for her to comment. (*Jean catches Tom as he moves away.*) Right – go back tomorrow. Can you go at 7.30 in the morning – see the boyfriend, the singer. Apparently he's younger, he can't want a kid hanging round the place.

POLICE CONSTABLE (*voice distorted*) Will do, ma'am.

JEAN Thank you.

Hardly has she put the phone down when Tom is heard ripping at the shelf. We watch Jean's face as she waits. Then at last the shelf crashes to the floor. She taps Tom's shoulder. He turns.

JEAN Kiss me.

He does. And stays close.

TOM (*mock-husky*) Think what I'm bringing you, Inspector, cork-tile ceilings, wall-to-wall toothpicks, micro-wave orchestras …

She kisses him.

JEAN Complete with extractors?

31 Jean's office (morning)

Blake roams while Jean sits.

BLAKE Last night, Inspector, I attended a meeting of the residents of the streets concerned. I reported on our conversation but they're threatening …

JEAN (*cold*) Councillor Blake, maps and directions for parking have already gone to their supporters' clubs –

BLAKE Inspector…

JEAN What I *have* done is get aid from my adjoining division, plus Mounted Branch and dogs –

BLAKE Those thugs –

JEAN – will be escorted from the coaches to the ground and from the ground back to the coaches. Every driver will be instructed on arrival his coach has to be out of the street by 5 pm. Any supporter found with a tin or bottle – it will be taken from him. (*She rises.*) Are you satisfied?

BLAKE How much is this going to cost the ratepayer!

JEAN (*crossing to the door*) Any barricades will have to be removed – so you think about that cost to the ratepayer. Your job is to inform the residents about all this, reassure them, if you will, over any arrangements and remind them of the cost of any unilateral action. Good morning.

BLAKE Good morning.
He moves out gracelessly; she follows.

32 The desk area

The phone is ringing as Blake marches through, followed by Jean.
BECK (*on the phone*) Hold the line. (*To Blake as he leaves.*) Bye, sir.
(*To Jean.*) Turley nick, ma'am.
JEAN (*taking the phone*) Inspector Darblay. Any luck?
TURLEY POLICE CONSTABLE (*voice distorted*) Negative again, ma'am.
JEAN Did you see the boyfriend?
POLICE CONSTABLE (*voice distorted*) Mr Mark Dancer – yes ma'am
– he said it was nowt to do with him.
JEAN What about her?
POLICE CONSTABLE (*voice distorted*) She's … very anti us now – we
got them out of bed.
JEAN I'm fascinated by the fact she's not worried. If I were her
I would have rung me. You checked the back?
POLICE CONSTABLE (*voice distorted*) Yes, ma'am. We could get the
night crime lads to do observations if they've got time.
JEAN No – no thank you. Will you tell your Detective Inspector
I'll probably be over there myself sometime.
POLICE CONSTABLE (*voice distorted*) Will do.
JEAN Thank you.
*She hands the phone back to Beck and stands immobile. Beck waits, then
slides a slip of paper towards her.*
BECK Then there's this, ma'am.
JEAN (*after she's read it*) If she rings again – I'll call round after
I've been to the Police Committee.

33 Kenny's room (afternoon)

*Mr Nicholas, in his dressing gown, is carefully finishing off tidying the
room. Everything is neat and in place. All that remains is for two pullovers now folded on the bed to be replaced. He crosses with them to the
wardrobe, presses down a shelf of shirts there and freezes. He pulls out
something – not the coin boxes, but a framed photograph of Pat Nicholas.
He looks at it gently, with no emotion showing. He replaces the frame
and lastly the pullovers and slowly closes the wardrobe.*

34 The Warden's office at the Home

Kay and Jean are sitting at Kay's desk; as usual, a jumble.

JEAN *Two* things?

KAY One of the bothers of running a shop like this is – what's concern and what's interference.

JEAN I know the problem –

KAY Yesterday – Carol said she visited her mother and didn't. I know because I checked. It was an excuse to go somewhere quite muddy and come back with her coat inside out.

JEAN Where?

Kay shrugs.

JEAN Then how do you know?

KAY I took her to and collected her from the County General – so before you slice my neck – you can see she wasn't allowed to run totally loose.

JEAN But she got away?

KAY (*nodding*) And brought back a flat parcel – which she said was her mother's. Obviously it wasn't. And I can't find it in her room.

JEAN How long was she away?

KAY An hour?

JEAN Then it must be in town here. Is she upstairs?

KAY She's gone with Ann and the small ones – swimming. Then (*she searches her desk top*) – where the hell is it? – she had a post-card this morning – just a "see you" – but she has no one!

JEAN (*alert*) From Turley?

KAY (*finding it*) Ah – (*she peers at the postmark*) Good heavens – how clever – yes!

JEAN Signed "Kenny"?

KAY (*looking*) No – "Coins".

She hands it over.

KAY Coins?

JEAN He's there! Thank you, Kay – you're an angel –

KAY A condition devoutly not to be wished.

JEAN (*reaching for the phone*) May I?

KAY (*nodding, troubled*) I'll have to give this to her –

JEAN (*as she dials*) That's all right – but keep an eye on that little lady.

BECK (*voice distorted*) Station Desk.

JEAN Sergeant Beck – listen. Tell Bentley to get into his civvies – he's coming out with me to Turley. I'll collect him in the car 7.15 sharp.

35   The Darblays' kitchen (late afternoon)

In total silence and very carefully Tom has painstakingly filled in the holes left by the tearing away of the shelving with plaster. He is in the process of completing the last one.
We hear Jean enter from the front door. It slams.
JEAN *(off)* Tom?
TOM Here.
She enters, already unbuttoning her uniform jacket, obviously in haste.
TOM Getting plastered.
JEAN Hm. Very neat.
TOM Thank you.
JEAN You're welcome.
Tom absently indicates with his trowel three sheets of tracing paper, with alternative kitchen designs on them.
TOM Take your pick.
As Jean quickly glances through them, Tom returns to his finishing.
TOM You can have the cooker there – fridge there, working top over it, with the washer in the corner, or top here next to a deep freeze, with the cooker there, and the washer next to the door – working tops in the gaps. (*He looks up and grins.*) Or you can do it yourself.
JEAN I'll talk to you later!

36   The desk area at the police station

Beck and Bentley are there. Jean enters. She is smart in a two piece suit. She looks startled at the waiting Bentley – who is so casual and near punk he's numb with embarrassment. He looks at her, then away. Pause.
JEAN We're not looking for an international drugs ring. Where *did* you get all that?
BENTLEY Saved up, ma'am.
Jean turns away to hide her rising laughter and – as she catches the eye of the broadly grinning Beck – this proves very difficult.
BENTLEY What are we going to do, ma'am?

JEAN Wait and watch. Come on.
They go.

37   Carol's room (early morning)

Beneath the barred window, Carol removes the coin box from the paper wrapper. Then, checking there is no sound from outside, she touches the coins with her fingertips, a study in wonder.

38   Rear of Mrs Nicholas's house (early evening)

Bentley on watch.
There is a quick movement and the rustle of "someone" in Mrs Nicholas's neighbour's hedge on the far side of the garden. Bentley, "on guard", frowns at the noise – he cannot see the side door on the hidden side of the house.
Bentley whistles. Jean has been checking the front of the house, and walks quickly back to Bentley.
BENTLEY (*nervous whisper*) Ma'am, I'm not sure, but I think I
    heard somebody on the far side, there. I could have gone
    over, but then it might not have been the boy. Sorry.
JEAN (*quietly*) For once you've done the right thing. If you're not
    sure, ever, seek advice. Whistle around here – that garage
    for a start – bins – everywhere.

39   Mrs Nicholas's hallway

The front doorbell "Avons", and again, as Mrs Nicholas appears, glass in hand, from the lounge area and pulls open the door.
PAT Yes?
JEAN I'm Inspector Darblay of the Hartley Police –
She shows her card.
PAT This is the third time. He's *not* here!
JEAN I have reason to believe he is.
She pushes in and closes the door.
PAT You've got a bloody nerve!
JEAN I'm not discussing police business on any doorstep in front
    of neighbours. Will you please go to the kitchen door –

PAT Give me one good reason –

JEAN The best – your concern for your boy.

PAT Yes – *my* boy!

JEAN That why you haven't lifted that phone once?

Pat slams her glass into Jean's hand and makes for the kitchen.

The camera stays on Jean. She places the drink by the telephone, which is under a large clubland blowup photograph of Mark Dancer – he looks flash.

PAT Come in, flatfoot!

JEAN Lock it – and bring the key.

We hear the kitchen door being locked and Pat and Bentley appear back in the hall.

JEAN (*taking the key*) Stay here. Watch the staircase while I do downstairs – and don't move.

PAT You're not going in my kitchen!

JEAN I'll look in every cupboard, paper bin, tap walls –

PAT Have you got a warrant!

JEAN When *Your* boy's missing?

PAT Why don't you get on to his dad!

JEAN We have.

She goes into the kitchen. Bentley stares up the empty stairs.

PAT Lucky you ever found him in – I hardly ever saw him in fifteen years of marriage.

40 Mrs Nicholas's stairs and landing

PAT It's not my fault I'm living here! You can't help being in love! Look at this and what I used to put up with – I *wanted* to take him from that court!

Jean emerges briskly from the lounge and motions Bentley to precede her.

PAT Why up there?

JEAN Mrs Nicholas –

PAT Why all this fuss for a kid who might just be having a night away from a pigsty? *I* did when I was his age –

JEAN (*quietly*) Because he might also be a thief.

This stops Mrs Nicholas, then she starts up the stairs before Jean.

On the landing Bentley reappears carrying a cane bathroom chair and proposes to stand on it to test the loft hatch.

PAT (*screaming*) Get off that!

She struggles with Bentley – who eventually wins, then removes his jacket to cover the chair. He stands on it and tests the trap door – it won't give. Before Jean can say anything Bentley gives it a hefty shove and it splinters upwards, disturbing the paint.

PAT That was painted over! For God's sake!

JEAN Up you go.

Tucking his torch in his shirt Bentley levers himself up and is lost in the darkness.

41   Inside the Home (evening)

Kay, doing her rounds, taps on Carol's door. There is no reply.

KAY Carol?

The light goes out under her door. Kay shrugs, waits then goes.

Carol in her anorak – reversed because it's darker – cautiously emerges onto the landing. She is carrying her "army" bag. She listens … Silence … Then makes for the stairs.

42   Mrs Nicholas's landing

Standing on the chair we see Bentley carefully replacing the loft cover. Then he picks up his coat and returns the chair to the bathroom.

43   Mrs Nicholas's bedroom

Pat stands, nervous, while Jean gets to her feet from looking under the bed. Bentley enters. Then Jean crosses to the wardrobe – opens it, and moves some shoes with her foot. Then she flicks the dresses and jackets along, and turns away.

PAT *(with a tinge of relief)* I've told you haven't I!

This makes Jean go back to the wardrobe and go along the dresses singly. One won't move. Then Kenny's head, grinning, appears up through the neck of a dress.

KENNY It wasn't her fault.

As he steps out, Pat starts slinging anything she can find at Jean.

PAT I wanted him here! He wanted to come! So I kept him!
(indicating the house) All this'll go 'cos I'm too old! But I don't
    want Kenny gone!

Bentley moves across and holds her, but she continues to struggle violently.

PAT I wanted him here! He's mine! Anything but back with that dead man!

Finally she gives up, sobbing.

PAT You can't get me on anything! I'm a mother.

JEAN Harbouring? Obstructing the police? But don't think I don't understand.

Kenny during this has removed the dress and hung it back neatly.

JEAN (*to Kenny*) Do *you* want to be here?

KENNY (*wry*) It's quieter.

He grins at Jean – as if looking for approval.

JEAN Come on, young man.

PAT *I'm coming!!*

JEAN Yes, you are.

44 Jean's office (night)

Bentley, carrying a tray of cups, enters with Sergeant Beck.

KENNY (*grinning*) How?

JEAN Carol.

KENNY She wouldn't say. Y'lying!

JEAN She was caught second time. You know that. That's why you ran. Now, we know what was taken. Where is it all now?

KENNY (*serious*) Y'haven't cautioned me. You've got to do that with an adult present.

JEAN We're not taking a statement yet. We're just talking.

Jean motions towards Kay, nervous in the corner.

JEAN But you're right. That's one of the reasons we've got Mrs Brown here.

Sergeant Beck, having served Jean then Kay, plonks a cup before Kenny.

BECK Where're your coins, lad?

Real shock shows on Kenny's face.

BECK They're not back at y'dad's place.

JEAN Are they with the rest?

Kenny ignores his tea.

JEAN If we don't find them, somebody else might. Even take them.

KENNY Can I go out and get them, then come back here?

JEAN No.

KENNY They're mine!

JEAN Those tins of food, cutlery, blankets, primus – they're Major Adams'.

Silence, then Kenny's face bursts into an infectious grin.

KENNY You're magic. I'll show you 'em. (*He stands up.*) You don't hear fighting there.

JEAN I'm going to caution you, Kenny.

KAY (*breaking in*) Is it where Carol may have run away to?

The camera turns to take in Pat's face – all the poise is gone. She's aghast at the seriousness of what's happening.

45   A small brick-lined room (night)

With heavy-duty torches, Jean, Pat, Bentley and Kenny reach (through a small aperture) a cosy, brick-lined "room", a kiln.

It is domestic – arranged with the food, primus, a box for a table with candles, a bed in the corner.

As they enter Carol springs from the bed. They all enter but Carol's eyes are only for Kenny.

KENNY Hello.

CAROL Why did you go away?

KENNY So we wouldn't get caught.

He is rummaging in a box.

KENNY (*whirling*) Where're m'coins!

CAROL Back at the Home. So you wouldn't get caught.

Pat looks at Jean.

46   Inside a police coach

The coach is parked in an industrial side street, perhaps facing a factory. Sitting towards the rear of the coach, and in deep foreground, are Bentley and another couple of policemen, helmets off, but waiting. The coach driver listens intently to the commentary and cheers of the football match coming over his radio. Jean steps up into the bus, and settles into the seat nearest the door. After a little while:

BENTLEY Everything all right, ma'am?

JEAN So far.

She doesn't look round.

Family Unit

Ian Kennedy Martin

The Cast

Inspector Jean Darblay

Tom Darblay

Sergeant Joseph Beck

Sergeant George Parrish

PC Roland Bentley

Sergeant Maggie Cullinane

Jennie Randall

Murphy

Maeve

Mrs Argent

Joss Buckle

Mr Jenks

Clerk of the Court

Magistrate

Court Usher

Hospital sister

Family Unit

1 Higham Street, Hartley

The episode opens on a derelict site, due for demolition. Jean drives up in her Mini, on her way to work. Something catches her eye and she stops nearby. She picks up her personal radio.

JEAN (*into radio*) Inspector Darblay to Hartley.

VOICE Yes, ma'am?

JEAN Is Sergeant Beck there?

VOICE Yes, he's here, ma'am.

JEAN Call him to the radio, please.

Jean gets out of her Mini, walks towards a row of houses – a poor street of two-up and two-downs.

BECK'S VOICE Sergeant Beck, ma'am.

JEAN Higham Street, number twenty one. Will you check it out, please, sergeant.

BECK'S VOICE Anything in particular you want checking, ma'am?

JEAN You'll see when you get there. I'm on my way in.

BECK'S VOICE Yes, ma'am.

Jean returns to her car and drives off.

2 The desk area of Hartley Police Station

As Jean enters the Hartley Station Parrish is covertly eating a bacon roll.

PARRISH 'Morning, ma'am.

JEAN 'Morning, George.

PARRISH One drunk and disorderly in the cells. Stole the yellow globe off a zebra crossing. John Michael Murphy.

JEAN Anything?

PARRISH We've seen him in here over the years. And your compassionate posting lady turned up ten minutes ago. I put her in your office.

JEAN What's she like?

PARRISH Nice smile, ma'am, an antidote on a nasty morning.

JEAN What's nasty about it?

PARRISH Had some Spanish white wine last night.

JEAN It doesn't go with bacon rolls.

PARRISH Outside the Costa Brava, ma'am, it doesn't go with anything.

JEAN Sergeant Beck on his way to Coleman Parade?

PARRISH Yes, ma'am.

JEAN If Bentley's around, could you ask him whether he could make two coffees?

PARRISH Right, ma'am.

Jean heads for her office.

3 Jean's office

As Jean walks in Sergeant Margaret (Maggie) Cullinane (in uniform) stands up. She's been four-and-a-half years in the force, which means a swift promotion to the rank, which makes her a very bright girl. She's just been on "the special course". Married, she lives in Preston. She's in Hartley on a compassionate posting because of her mother who lives in the town.

JEAN Morning.

MAGGIE Morning, ma'am. I'm Sergeant Margaret Cullinane.

Jean indicates that she should sit.

Maggie does so.

Jean studies the girl.

Maggie has an easy smile. There's a certain (pleasant enough) sharpness in some of Maggie's responses.

JEAN Compassionate posting? What's the problem?

MAGGIE My mother's to undergo a hip replacement operation, Hartley Cottage Hospital tomorrow. She's sixty-nine. I wasn't going to make a request for a compassionate posting. My Chief Superintendent actually insisted, ma'am.

JEAN How long will you be here, d'you reckon?

MAGGIE If all goes well, a few days – if it doesn't, maybe a fortnight, maybe more. It's her second operation. The first one didn't take.

JEAN Sergeant Parrish will explain the ropes to you and which ones to pull, and which ones not to, and why and when. There's just one point I'd like to make. We had a particular secondment here who criticised everything the previous shift got up to. D'you think you could avoid that – criticising the activities of the previous shift?

MAGGIE I'm not here to make any trouble, ma'am.

Jean studies her.

JEAN How long have you been in the Service?

MAGGIE Four-and-a-half years.

JEAN You had a fast promotion. Are you ambitious?

MAGGIE Yes, ma'am.

JEAN Where do you see your future in the Service?

MAGGIE I want your job.

JEAN To be in charge of a section?

MAGGIE I spent my teenage years in Hartley. I want to be in charge of *this* section, ma'am.

Jean's amused and mildly challenged.

JEAN You're very blunt. I'm the incumbent here, and here I stay, for the foreseeable.

MAGGIE We can never tell what's going to happen to our futures in the service, ma'am. Can we?

JEAN See if you can find Constable Bentley. Tell him we're still waiting for our coffee will you?

MAGGIE Yes, ma'am.

Maggie exits. The telephone goes. Jean picks it up.

JEAN (*into phone*) Yes? What d'you mean, he doesn't know what he's doing? I'll come out.

She replaces phone and exits.

4 Higham Street

Beck stands by the corrugated iron sheets that cover up the front door of number twenty one Higham Street.

JEAN'S VOICE Sergeant Beck?

BECK Yes, ma'am.

JEAN What is it?

BECK (*into radio*) I'm here at front door of twenty one Higham Street, as you instructed. It's boarded up as you know. What am I supposed to be doing here?

JEAN'S VOICE Sergeant Beck. Leave the front door and walk across the street.

BECK (*into radio*) Yes, ma'am.

He walks across the street.

JEAN'S VOICE Are you over the street?

BECK (*into radio*) Yes, ma'am.
JEAN'S VOICE Look up.
Beck looks up. We see his point of view. There is a thin trickle of smoke coming out of the chimney of the boarded-up house.
BECK Oh, I see, ma'am. Smoke!

5 The radio room of the police station

JEAN (*into mike*) Exactly. Now, find out why there's smoke coming out of that chimney, although the house is boarded up.
BECK'S VOICE Yes, ma'am.
JEAN No smoke without fire, sergeant.
PARRISH No, ma'am.

6 Inside the cell at Hartley Police Station

JEAN John Michael Murphy, are you prepared to sign the charge sheet and be bailed?
MURPHY If you're prepared to recognise the six counties as part of the Republic of Ireland.
JEAN No, we're not prepared to do that, Mr Murphy.
MURPHY What's your name, miss? I'll want it if I'm going to be lodging a complaint against my treatment here.
JEAN My name's Inspector Darblay.
MURPHY (*triumphant*) I thought it was. You're the one who's married to Tom Darblay, aren't you? (*grim*) And I've certainly heard about you, miss...
JEAN Are you prepared to sign the charge sheet and be bailed? Yes or no?
MURPHY Of course I'll sign it. I'll sign anything to get out of here.
JEAN Your court appearance is on the fourteenth. Don't forget it.
MURPHY I won't forget it. (*veiled threat*) And I won't forget you. (*She turns and exits.*) Poor Tom Darblay. You trapped a very decent man...a very decent man.

7 The rear of number twenty one Higham Street

Sergeant Beck arrives, sees an open window and climbs through. Once inside he goes to the front of the house.

8 The front room of number twenty one

The camera shows us Maeve Murphy. She's fifteen-and-a-half. She'd be good-looking if it wasn't for some bad facial bruises. She's wearing a cheap sleeveless dress. Bruises can be seen on her arms. The dark room is illuminated only by the fire she's made of bits of wood, in the grate. She stands against the wall, terrified at Beck's approaching growls, then footsteps. Beck enters.

BECK (*kindly note*) So who are you, then? What are you doing trespassing here? (*Maeve, frightened, says nothing. Beck tries to be more informal, sympathetic.*) What's your name?

Maeve says nothing.

BECK Well, love, I must know your name. Are you going to tell me here or down the police station?

MAEVE Maeve Murphy.

BECK Address?

MAEVE Thirty-nine, Salford Road, Hartley.

BECK You wouldn't happen to be the daughter of John Murphy at the moment in police custody?

Maeve says nothing.

BECK Is John Murphy your dad?

MAEVE Yes.

BECK Now where did these bruises come from?

The girl's silent.

BECK You'd better come along with me.

MAEVE I don't want to.

BECK I'm sorry, love, but I think you ought to be seen by a doctor, or our police surgeon. You come along with me now.

MAEVE I can't walk proper. He kicked me ankle and I think me other knee's twisted.

She tries to step forward from where she's been leaning against the wall. She gives out a little cry and nearly falls.

BECK Who kicked your ankle? Who's done this to you? Was it your dad?

She says nothing.

9 The desk area of Hartley Police Station

Bentley is seen approaching Parrish carrying a coffee for Parrish. Parrish is filling in the desk diary.

PARRISH Put it down there.

BENTLEY Sarge, I don't think I should have to make the coffees for you, ma'am, Sergeant Beck, and all the visitors.

Parrish looks up, grim.

PARRISH (*harsh and sinister*) Is this mutiny, lad?

BENTLEY Sarge, the clerk should make the coffee. I mean, I think it's not right for me to be ferrying cups around, that's not why I joined the Force, to make coffee.

PARRISH (*flat*) Is this revolution? Is that why you joined the Force – to undermine an entire system which has been built, for the last hundred and fifty years, around tea and coffee breaks?

BENTLEY I just don't think I should make the coffees and teas.

PARRISH Roland, now you know we never *order* you to make teas or coffee, we ask if you would like to, and of course you volunteer. Shall I do you a favour, lad?

BENTLEY What's that, Sarge?

PARRISH I'll pretend I haven't heard any of this. I want to put a question to you. Think very hard before you answer.

PARRISH Where are the bloody biscuits?

BENTLEY There's none left, Sarge.

Parrish brings out of his pocket a handful of change, sets thirty pence on desk.

PARRISH Show us a fast clean pair of heels down the High Street. What's the point of your rotten coffee without any biscuits. (*sharp*) Move.

Bentley, frustrated look, takes money and goes.

Desk telephone rings.

PARRISH (*into phone*) Station desk. Yes, Joe. No, he's just off, five minutes ago, bailed...hang on, I'll have you put through.

10   Jean's office

The phone rings, and Jean answers.

JEAN Yes. Yes, Sergeant Beck?

11   A hospital corridor

BECK I got into twenty-one Higham Street. There was a young girl inside, name Maeve Murphy, daughter of John just bailed. She's been beaten up badly. She won't say it's her father that did it, but I think he did. I've taken her to Hartley Cottage Hospital. A social worker at the hospital says the family is known to Social Services. So I put a call through to check. One of the social workers who deals with the Murphy family is known to you, ma'am.

Intercut with Jean's office.

JEAN Who's that, sergeant?

BECK It's your husband, ma'am.

A short, thoughtful pause by Jean.

JEAN Stay put. I'll see if I can have a word with Mr Darblay and come down there.

12 An office at social services

The camera shows us a bleak, small room, where Tom Darblay sits taking some notes, his notepad on his knees.

Old Mrs Argent is sitting on the edge of a chair.

TOM Can I ask what age you are, Mrs Argent?

MRS ARGENT Sixty-five. My husband's forty-nine. You see, I married him when I was thirty-five years old. He were nineteen at the time. Now I'm an old woman and he's a young-looking forty-nine-year-old.

TOM Look, you've been together a long time, you and your husband. I think you should be very certain you haven't mislaid the pension book somewhere before you start telling police he's pinched it.

MRS ARGENT But I don't have a penny.

TOM Yes, all right – well I'm coming to that.

The door opens.

Jennie Randall, a senior social worker, enters.

As a probationer, Tom has been "allocated" to Jennie – meaning that, for his first three months in the social services, he'll work close to her (before he branches out on his own) and his work will be closely supervised by her.

JENNIE Excuse me. Tom, can I have a word.

TOM I think we should be able to get you some money to carry on. Can you just give me a minute.

MRS ARGENT Oh, ta, love.

Tom crosses to Jennie.

JENNIE I've had your wife on the phone – in her official capacity. There's a problem with the John Murphy case.

TOM What?

JENNIE She's not sure. But it looks like Murphy's beaten his daughter up. I have to attend a legal briefing, so I suggested you deal with it – you know the background. Fill Jean in with the details and go with her to the hospital.

TOM I haven't finished with Mrs Argent yet, you know.

JENNIE What's the problem?

TOM Well, her husband's left her. He's taken money from her tea caddy and she thinks he's gone off with her pension book. And if she's no money she'll need some money by the end of the week.

JENNIE I'll deal with it.

Tom introduces her to Mrs Argent.

TOM Mrs Argent, this is Jennie Randall. She's our Senior Social Worker. I have to go to the Cottage Hospital.

MRS ARGENT Oh dear.

TOM I'm going to ask Jennie here to finish sorting out your problem.

Tom hands his notes to Jennie.

JENNIE Do sit down, Mrs Argent.

TOM I'll see you later.

MRS ARGENT Aye, love.

Tom exits.

JENNIE Now I believe your husband's left you.

MRS ARGENT It's the first time.

13 Jean's office

TOM Jennie Randall's always dealt with the Murphy family. I've met him three times. Six months ago Murphy's wife, Margaret, died. That left him with four to bring up. All girls – age range five-and-a-half to fifteen-and-a-half. Original problem seems to stem from an industrial accident, led to terrible migraines. Since then he's only been able to do light work.

JEAN Fracturing jaws? Breaking up pubs?

TOM I'm being serious, Jean.

JEAN So am I. We've known him for years.

TOM Look, how easy d'you think it is for a man like that to adapt to the death of a wife and suddenly be dumped with four kids to bring up?

JEAN Should be a sobering experience. At 4 a.m. this morning he was blind drunk, smashing the globe off a zebra crossing.

TOM Well, he's not very bright. He has to bring up four kids unaided. Of course on occasion he's going to turn to drink.

JEAN It looks like he's beaten up his daughter. That has to be my first concern.

TOM Well, let's go and see the damage, see whether it is really down to him.

14 Section of a hospital ward

The camera moves into close-up on Maeve lying half propped up in bed, face bruised, some dressings over the bruising on her arms. After a moment the camera pulls back to include Jean.

Sergeant Beck is standing behind her. Tom is standing off ten feet away by a door.

JEAN You're all right?

MAEVE Yes.

JEAN Is there anything you want?

MAEVE No, I'm fine. Thanks.

JEAN All right, love, you just rest. (*The camera tracks with her over to the door. She talks quietly to Tom so that Maeve can't overhear*) I call that a vicious beating. So does the doctor.

TOM She hasn't said it's her father.

JEAN I think she'd tell us who it was if it was anybody other than her father. She intimated to Sergeant Beck it was Murphy. *If* I can prove it was him, then I'm going to take action.

TOM What action?

JEAN Well, I'll talk to Murphy. I'll check out the other children. If I don't like what I see, I may be forced to remove them to a´"place of safety".

Jean goes out to the corridor. Tom follows.

TOM Hey, wait, Jean. Look. I don't know this case well. Jennie Randall's always dealt with the Murphys. I think the least you can do is talk to her. Look, I know this man is struggling to adjust to the death of his wife. He's not bright. He needs a helluva lot of constructive help.

JEAN My first concern has to be with this child and the other Murphy children.

TOM All right. Let's talk about Maeve. She's doing a terrific job

71

as a substitute mother, feeding the kids, getting them up in the morning, getting them off to school. Now you're not going to crash in and scupper that with a quick removal order, get them into a council-approved care home – they've lost their mother, now you're not going to tear them away from their dad.

JEAN (*gently*) Hey!

TOM What?

JEAN What's happening here? Why are we arguing?

TOM I think your approach is a little bit unsubtle.

JEAN Is it?

TOM Yes.

JEAN I think Murphy's a regular drunkard. He may get drunk again, hit her again. I'll check the state of the other children and if I don't like what I see, I *have* to do something about it. The appropriate action, to remove the possibility of his attacking his daughter again, is an order to place the kids in care for a few days while we sort him and the situation out.

TOM Well I know Jennie Randall and on the basis of what we have so far, she's not going to allow you to break up this family. And I'll probably support her in that.

JEAN (*put out, and somehow put down*) Sergeant Beck will take me back to the station. I'll see you later.

TOM Right.

He heads off.

Jean heads back towards the hospital ward.

15 The Green Elm pub

We watch Tom entering one of Murphy's known haunts.

Murphy, head bowed over a Guinness, is in the corner.

Tom goes over to him.

TOM Morning, John.

MURPHY Oh, Mr Darblay. I saw your wife this morning. She's like a kind of cruel penguin in the uniform. How did you end up married to that one – begging your pardon?

TOM Why the hell did you hit Maeve last night?

MURPHY You know I didn't remember about that until I got out of nick. I was going down the road and suddenly the whole thing came back to me – (*groans*) Oh, God...

TOM What happened?

MURPHY (*upset*) Well last night...I usually go from the pub straight to my night-watchman job at the bakery. Well, last night I come home, found her, found my daughter Maeve, fifteen she is, in her bedroom playing her records to some class of an Asian or Pakistani. I tried to grab him. He was off like greased lightning. (*pause*) I hit her. I shouldn't have. But I couldn't contain the anger coming up from my guts into my brain. I mean, if I hadn't come home, I know the next step would be for him to seduce her to bed. I saw red.

TOM You'd better go and talk to her.

MURPHY I'll be going home at dinner. She'll be there feeding the kids.

TOM She's in Hartley Cottage Hospital. (*The camera stays on Murphy, clearly upset*) Now look, John, let's get this quite clear, on the basis of what you've done so far, the police may well go to court to get a care order to take your kids away from you.

MURPHY They can't do that.

TOM They might try. They may succeed. I'm warning you. Any more problems and it will be court. Just finish the drink and go to the hospital now.

MURPHY How can I face her? You know Maeve. She's the one that keeps the whole bloody family together – since Margaret died.

TOM I know.

MURPHY It was that little cocoa bastard. And because I couldn't get him, I turned on her.

16 The hospital corridor

Tom and Murphy have met the ward sister

TOM Not here. What do you mean, she's not here?

SISTER I'm sorry. We sent her down to have her foot X-rayed, and obviously after that she just dressed herself and walked out.

MURPHY She'll have gone to her friends.

TOM (*to the Sister*) Thank you. (*to Murphy*) What friends?

MURPHY I don't know. She's got lots of friends.

TOM Come on, I'd better take you home.

MURPHY I don't need you to take me home.

TOM Look, now you've got my number – phone me at the office as soon as you've talked to her. Right?

MURPHY Hey, what happened to Miss Randall? Miss Randall usually deals with me.

TOM She had to be somewhere else. She'll be in touch. Keep off the drink.

MURPHY I won't touch any drink now. Not after last night.

17 Beside a canal

We watch Maeve and her three sisters, Maureen, five-and-a-half, Coleen, seven-and-a-half, and Megan, ten.

They wander along the side of the canal, the younger children eating fruit.

MAEVE Listen to me. When you get home this afternoon, I won't be in – right? But I'll come in about midnight when Dad's at work. And before you go to bed remember to wash your ears and clean your teeth and mind, you lot – no fighting … do you hear me? Maureen come here – don't run.

18 The Green Elm pub

It is 2.30 p.m. Murphy is with his drinking pal, Joss Buckle, a sixty-year-old local man.

MURPHY I've got to find Maeve, Joss. Stop her from getting into trouble with the police. You know that social worker, Tom Darblay, fine man, would you believe married to that witch that female Inspector…he says police might take my kids away from me. No chance. What time you got, Joss?

JOSS (*looking at his watch*) Twenty-five after two.

MURPHY Another drink. Your round.

JOSS Landlord Boot says he'll not serve us wi' another.

MURPHY (*amused*) Is that his name, Boot?

JOSS Mister Boot to you, John. Or Boot Esquire.

JOSS (*stirring it*) I'd like to be there with you when you find your daughter. I want to see you bow and scrape to her for clouting her because she was about to get in sheets with a little brown monkey.

MURPHY I shouldn't have hit her.

JOSS That's right. You've already got four kids to bring up, what difference does it make if another little'un comes along.

MURPHY (*very drunk and thoughtful*) I've got to find that monkey. You know he's the one who's responsible for all of this! And I know where he comes from...

JOSS Pakistan.

Murphy gives Joss a withering look.

MURPHY I'm going to descend on him, mangle him and give him a biblical pasting.

JOSS You're going to hit him?

MURPHY I feel very bad Joss, very low. Why did I get this fate? I've had about as much as I can stand. I'm tired of it all, Joss, and angry. I feel this great anger about me since Margaret died. I feel I have to hit back Joss. Or go under. Because I feel I'm going under. Sinking. Sinking...I know where to find that little gringo!

19   Jean's office

Sergeant Maggie Cullinane knocks and enters on Jean, who's working on some papers.

JEAN Yes?

MAGGIE Murphy's not at home. Maeve neither. The three kids turned up after school – said they had a picnic lunch with Maeve. She told them she'd be back late evening when the father is at his nightwatchman duties.

JEAN Right.

MAGGIE I've checked at the bakery. And I've left word for them to phone us as soon as Murphy arrives.

JEAN Good. Any news on your mother?

MAGGIE Operation 7 a.m. tomorrow.

JEAN I hope all goes well.

MAGGIE Thank you, ma'am.

20   Jennie Randall's office

Tom and Jennie Randall are at their tea break

JENNIE Look, I hate to have to say this, but we're just going to have to deal with the issues as raised with the Murphy case. I can't allow Jean's involvement to influence us.

TOM She's worried about me appearing in court.

JENNIE Yes, well you are involved with the case. Now the police concern is Murphy beat up his daughter, might do it again, and has three other motherless children floating about. I can say I know John Murphy and I know he didn't beat Maeve because he hates her, or because he's mad or dangerous. He gets on reasonably well with his kids. He's a kid himself. It's his great saving grace. Your wife's wrong, Tom. And if she goes into court with the Murphy family, I'm going into court to fight her. And I'm afraid I'll have to ask you to come and help me.

The camera settles on Tom. This is a serious situation that's developing between him and Jean.

21 Row of semi-detacheds (early evening)

The camera shows us a row of semi-detacheds on one side of a street. On the other side we see the beginnings of a few acres of common.

A bus comes down the street, halts at a stop, lets off a few passengers, and moves on.

One is a sixteen-year-old Asian lad. He crosses the road towards the houses.

From a window of one of them Maeve sees him coming – they wave to each other.

She goes downstairs to meet him as he moves to the front of the house.

An animal roar makes the boy turn.

MURPHY Hey, you … come here. I wanna talk to you. I'll kill you, I'll kill you.

Before the boy can take to his heels, Murphy's on top of him, grabs him, wrestles him clumsily.

Maeve comes out of the front door – sees what's happening.

MAEVE Da …Da … don't!

And suddenly the fifteen-year-old daughter has rushed in, crazily clawing at her father's face with her finger-nails. Murphy bellows in pain and rage. The little Asian is out from under Murphy and off and sprinting across the road, onto the common and away.

Murphy grapples with Maeve.

MURPHY You whore! You whore!

We move into very close shot, looking at the top of Murphy's head and body. His face, incensed, is facing the camera, as once again he attacks his daughter.

22   The same street of semi-detacheds (later)

We see the street from another angle and take in Jean's Mini.
Jean is alone in it. She comes fast down the road, pulls into the kerb behind a police car, and an ambulance.
Maeve is being helped by Sergeant Beck and two ambulance men into the ambulance.
Jean gets out of her Mini, and we stay in long shot while she has a brief word with Maeve and Beck. Maeve is put into ambulance and the rear doors close.
Jean walks away with Beck, as the ambulance takes off.
We move in to hear them.

JEAN What about the three other kids?

BECK A neighbour's taken them in.

JEAN We'd better organise bringing them in. What happened to Murphy?

BECK Last seen he shot off down the street.

JEAN He must be found.

BECK Yes, ma'am.

JEAN Well I'm going off watch. I'll be at home. Phone me when you get him, or the children to the station – Sergeant Cullinane will give you a hand with the children.

BECK Yes, ma'am.

She heads back to the Mini, Beck to the area car.
Jean drives off.

23   The corner of a ward, Hartley Cottage Hospital

Maeve is shown back in bed in the same ward. The ward is in semi-darkness and Maeve is sedated and asleep.
Tom and Jean stand at the foot of her bed. They're silent. After a moment they turn and leave.

24   The kitchen of the Darblays' house (same night)

Tom and Jean come in.
Tom takes off his coat.
Jean doesn't, and just sits down.

TOM Coffee? (*She shakes her head. He goes and fills the kettle for him-*

self. We sense a stiffness in the atmosphere – there's going to be a row now – but they'll keep their voices down. They care a great deal for each other but they have arrived at a rare occasion of conflict over principle.

TOM (*making an effort to talk quietly, gently*) I talked to Jennie Randall.

JEAN When?

TOM Before the hospital.

JEAN And?

TOM I told her Murphy had attacked Maeve again. Drunk. I told her you were pretty set on going to court.

JEAN "Pretty set"?

TOM She reiterated that a man losing his wife six months ago, faced with the prospect of bringing up four kids broke, is bound to go to pieces, get drunk. Hit out. But she thinks to take the kids away from him will destroy him, finish him, and the kids, and the family, finally.

JEAN She thinks – what do you think?

TOM Just let me finish. She'll resist any attempt by you to start any process of breaking up the family unit. And she expects me to assist her.

JEAN What do you think?

TOM Well I'm inclined to agree with her. I know Murphy – not a bad man. Until he's drunk. That's not a regular occurrence. He drinks regularly. He doesn't get blind drunk regularly.

JEAN Now let's get this straight. After what happened to Maeve Murphy this evening I shall be forced to go to court immediately for a twenty-eight-day order. What you're saying is that you will also be in that court assisting Jennie Randall against me.

TOM When I joined Social Services I was tagged onto a Senior Social Worker, Jennie Randall. It's my job to assist her.

JEAN …When you joined Social Services implicit in the support I gave you to do that was the obvious understanding that the job was not going to end up on a collision course with me and my job.

TOM Look, Jean…yours is not the only…

JEAN I haven't finished. It's possible a local journalist will be hanging around the court. It'll make a good story for him won't it? "Husband social worker opposes wife police inspec-

tor in court battle…" It'll sound great back at my headquarters.

TOM Jennie Randall will be opposing you.

JEAN I don't want you in court, Tom.

TOM Well I may have to be.

JEAN Explain to Jennie the situation and tell her to get another
assistant.

TOM (*quietly, firm*) No, I'm sorry. I've been visiting the Murphy
family. I'm the obvious person to be assisting her.

JEAN I'm asking you to walk away from this, Tom. I want you
to tell Jennie Randall to get some other assistant.

TOM No, I can't.

JEAN A matter of principle, is it – is that what you're saying?

TOM Yes it is. (*Jean gets up, picks up her coat, and then makes for the
door*) Where are you going?

JEAN Back to the station.

TOM You're off duty, for God's sake.

JEAN I want to think. I'll think more clearly away from here.
(*pause*)

She goes out.

25   The desk area of Hartley Police Station

*Sergeant Maggie is leaving, but she reacts to seeing a light in Jean's office
and goes to investigate.*

26   Jean's office

*We watch Jean sitting at her desk, chin cupped in her hands, depressed.
Sergeant Maggie makes a quiet entrance through the door which was ajar,
sees that Jean is upset before Jean can change her expression.*

MAGGIE I'm sorry, ma'am. (*for interrupting*)

JEAN All right.

(*beat*)

MAGGIE Is there anything the matter, ma'am?

There's a long pause.

JEAN (*with feeling*) Bloody men.

Maggie, for a moment makes no comment. Then

MAGGIE There's no sign of Murphy. He was expected on shift

at the bakery factory nine-thirty. He's not there. Shall I put someone on watch there, ma'am?

JEAN I don't think he'll turn up for work tonight.

MAGGIE I met the next door family who are looking after the kids. They're very nice.

JEAN Good.

MAGGIE I've left word with the late shift bakery foreman to contact if Murphy, or his sparring partner, Mulvany, turn up before he goes off.

JEAN Right.

The camera rests on Maggie, concerned for Jean.

MAGGIE Is there anything else I can do for you, ma'am?

JEAN Just impress on everyone that Murphy must be found.

MAGGIE Yes, ma'am.

She goes out. We focus in on Jean, still upset.

27   Prosser's Fast Foods bakery (night)

We are in a large "factory" style room, obviously devoted to bakery on a large scale. In the corner, there is a small office.

Murphy reels in carrying a bottle of scotch. He weaves his way to the office, slumps in a chair, and swigs from his bottle.

He gets up to survey the scene. He spots a piece of machinery and it gives him an idea.

MURPHY (*softly*) That's it – custard!

He collects a large bucket or pan and crosses to the machine. He switches it on, places a pan under the pump handle and proceeds to pump a quantity of custard into the pan.

28   Outside the Darblays' house

A battered Austin Princess comes up the street. Murphy's driving. He pulls the car in and collides with the kerb, the car mounting the kerb. He brakes, gets out, goes round to the rear of the car, opens the boot.

The camera pans round to see, twenty feet away, Jean's Mini. We are in the street of the Darblays' house. The lights are out in the Darblays' house. Pan back to Murphy who has got the very large pot of custard out of the boot, and now staggers forward and up the street to Jean's Mini. There's total silence, and apart from Murphy, no movement in the street. Murphy reaches the Mini, and with a huge effort lifts the pot onto the roof, up-turning it. Gallons of custard spread out and over, and down the car. Murphy helps the spreading process along with his big hands, a triumphant expression on his drunken face.

29 The same road the next day

The camera shows us a close-up of Tom Darblay, then pulls back. He's standing on the kerb outside his house studying the custard-encrusted Mini. He turns, heads back and round the side of the house to enter the kitchen.

30 The kitchen of the Darblays' home

As Tom enters Jean comes in from hall door, spruce in her uniform. They have not reconciled anything overnight. They're still upset with each other.

TOM (*flat*) Did you intend to use your Mini to drive to the court?

JEAN There's no parking there. Sergeant Beck's collecting me. Why?

TOM Oh. Nothing.

JEAN I'm going to ask you a last time – will you ask Jennie Randall to let you off going to court?

TOM Look I've been a visitor to the Murphy family. I'm the obvious person to be there.

JEAN (*cold and angry*) See you in court.

TOM Yes.

Tom exits.

31 Jennie Randall's office

We are in close up watching a shattered Tom.

TOM I don't believe it.

The camera pulls back to include Jennie Randall feverishly going through her filing cabinet trying to locate the "Dana Fox" file.

JENNIE I don't have a lot of time. This kid, Dana Fox – I've been seeing her for years – they think she took an overdose, an hour ago. She won't confirm or deny it. They've got the drug bottle with the label torn off – she won't say what was in it. They think I'm the only person she'll speak to.

TOM (*grim*) Look, do you expect me to go into that court alone and oppose my wife?

81

JENNIE I'm sorry, Tom. (*The desk buzzer goes*) That'll be the car. Tom, you have to do it.
We are left looking at the bewildered Tom.

32 Outside the Court

The police car is parked outside the juvenile court building which is behind Hartley Town Hall. Beck behind the wheel, Jean with him.
JEAN There's Tom.
Tom, Maeve and the three young kids cross the road from the car park towards the court.
Jean and Beck can be seen studying various other people milling around the steps and then going into the building.
JEAN Where's Jennie Randall then?
BECK I don't see no Collinson or any other local press.
JEAN God, I hope there's no journalists.
BECK Good luck, ma'am.
Jean gets out of the car, heads into the court.

33 Juvenile courtroom

This juvenile court is in a room more like a large office than the usual oak panelled courtroom.
CLERK I realise your problem, Mr Jenks, but I'm afraid we can't hold up proceedings.
JENKS I appreciate that.
Facing the bench, Tom and Jenks stand talking quietly to Maeve.
Jean enters, crosses to the bench and sits.
The court usher stands by lower doorway. At another table is the court clerk, near to the bench.)
COURT USHER All stand in court. (*All in the courtroom stand. Three magistrates enter – two elderly men, an early-middle-aged lady. They take their seats behind the bench – the lady in the middle*) Be seated.
COURT CLERK Your worships, number one on the court sheet – an application for an interim care order in respect of Maeve Murphy, Maureen Mary Murphy, Coleen Anne Murphy and Megan Louise Murphy. The application is by the police.
The lower door opens and Murphy appears, to the obvious surprise of all concerned.
The usher indicates to him to join Tom and Maeve.

Murphy makes his way self-consciously over to them. He has shaved and obviously made an effort to sober up and present a favourable image to the court.

He sits next to Maeve and in front of Tom.

Tom leans over to him.

TOM (*whisper*) Where the hell have you been?

MURPHY (*blandly*) I've been around.

The court clerk turns to the Social Services Solicitor.

COURT CLERK Mr Jenks, you are representing Social Services who are opposing this application?

SOCIAL SERVICES SOLICITOR Yes, your worships. (*He sits*)

COURT CLERK Inspector Darblay, you are making the application?

Jean stands

JEAN Yes, your worships.

COURT CLERK (*to Jean*) Are the parents in court?

JEAN Your worships, the father, John Michael Murphy, has just arrived. (*She nods to indicate Murphy*) The mother is deceased.

COURT CLERK Are the children in court?

JEAN Yes, your worships. The eldest child, Maeve Murphy, fifteen-and-a-half years of age, is present before the court. The other three children Maureen Mary Murphy, five-years-old, Coleen Anne Murphy, seven-years-old and Megan Louise Murphy, ten-years-old are in the court waiting room, and have been identified to the court. It is felt that their presence in this court, witnessing these proceedings, might be distressing for them.

COURT CLERK (*turning to the magistrates*) With your worships' permission.

CHAIRMAN Yes, very well. Do you agree, Mr Jenks?

SOCIAL SERVICES SOLICITOR Yes, Your worships.

COURT CLERK Maeve Murphy, please stand. (*Maeve stands*) You are Maeve Murphy, of thirty-nine Salford Road, Hartley?

MAEVE Yes sir.

COURT CLERK (*to Maeve*) you may be seated. (*To Jean*) We understand that your application is for a twenty-eight-day order to place these children into the care of the Local Authority whilst further enquiries are made.

JEAN Yes, your worships.

COURT CLERK Will you give us the reasons for your application?

Jean rises. Reading from a report.

JEAN The circumstances of this application, your worships, are

83

as follows: There are four children, Maeve Murphy aged fifteen years, Maureen Mary Murphy five years, Coleen Anne Murphy seven years, and Megan Louise Murphy ten years, who live at...

Jean has sat down – she is obviously puzzled and upset by the absence of Jennie Randall.

The Social Services Solicitor is now addressing the bench.

SOCIAL SERVICES SOLICITOR As Inspector Darblay states, there is no contention that these two assaults took place, but we believe, as does Maeve Murphy, that whilst there was no complete excuse for John Murphy's behaviour, there were certain mitigating circumstances and we'd like to call John Michael Murphy to the stand.

COURT CLERK John Michael Murphy, please.

All in court look round to Murphy, who stands and moves towards the table indicated by court clerk.

SOCIAL SERVICES SOLICITOR Mr Murphy, would you tell the magistrates a little about your family circumstances, and the death of your wife?

The camera turns to Murphy.

He has suddenly a clear-eyed look of competence. He talks easily, fluently and seriously – and impressively.

MURPHY My wife died six months ago. She left me with four little ones, aged five-and-a-half to fifteen-and-a-half. She was a rare woman, a good mother, a hard worker. She was in work at Durkin's Wool Company when she died, so her death was not only a dire hammer-blow of fate, it was also a loss of income to us. I am employed as nightwatchman at Prossor's Fast Foods. I have worked that place four years. In four years I have not taken from the state unemployment benefit that a lot of people do, being conscientious about wanting to work me living, and not ever a skivver.

SOCIAL SERVICES SOLICITOR Mr Murphy, can you tell the court what happened two nights ago when you returned to your home before going to your nightwork at the food company?

MURPHY I found my daughter, Maeve, in her bedroom, but not in bed though, with some form of a young Asian... (*Murphy continues his statement*) ...and the Asian was off and out of the house before I could collar him. As I was trying to get at him, my daughter was fighting to get me off, and somehow it ended up, the boy was gone, and I hitting her.

COURT CLERK Mr Murphy, I have to warn you to be careful

about what you're saying, as anything you say can later be used in evidence in proceedings against you.

Despite the warning, Murphy carries on.

MURPHY You see, it's not that I hate my children, it's that I love them. But I have this terrible anger born the hour that my Margaret died. It is as if my mind is going to blow up at any moment with my huge fear for my future, for the future of these children. I am here. I have four kids. I have not enough money. I can't meet my obligations. I see no solutions. Except to hang on for dearest life, me to my kids, and me and my kids, hang on to the raft and ride out the storm that will only end I think, when I am dead, and they are older.

SOCIAL SERVICES SOLICITOR Thank you, Mr Murphy

Murphy turns, goes back to his seat and sits down.

Cut to the magistrates.

They seem impressed by Murphy's performance.

CLERK Mr Jenks have we any report from the Social Services on this family?

SOCIAL SERVICES SOLICITOR Yes, your worships. Mr Tom Darblay is here.

LADY MAGISTRATE Darblay?

CLERK You are Mr Tom Darblay of the Hartley Social Services Department?

TOM I am.

CLERK May we have your report?

TOM The Social Services Department first became involved with the Murphy family several years ago, seven to be precise. The original difficulties for the family started the year after Mr Murphy's industrial accident ...

34 An anteroom to the court

The magistrates have ordered a brief "We will now retire" coffee break. Jean (standing ten feet away from Maeve) is in one corner of the anteroom. Murphy is in the opposite corner, talking to the Social Services Solicitor.

Tom's not there.

Maggie enters, crosses to Jean.

MAGGIE I phoned hospital.

JEAN How is your mother?

MAGGIE (*pleased*) She's out of anaesthetic, operation went fine.

Doctor says, no problem with her heart and the anaesthesia
...

JEAN That's good to hear. Those kids all right?

MAGGIE Yes – yes they're all right. How's Murphy doing?

JEAN He's a better actor than Laurence Olivier. (*Tom comes out of court*) Excuse me. (*she crosses to Tom*) What the hell happened to Jennie Randall?

TOM She couldn't come. She's got involved with an attempted suicide.

JEAN (*upset*) It looks good, doesn't it, you and me directly opposing each other.

TOM I'm sorry.

JEAN I don't think you are.

She turns to go.

TOM Wait. You're not going to bring up the business of the custard over your car are you? (*Jean says nothing*) What relevance has it to a man who's trying to hold his family together?

JEAN I've no proof it was Murphy.

TOM (*a touch mollified*) Thanks.

He goes back to the Murphy corner.

Jean goes back to Maggie.

JEAN I think we're going to lose this case...

35 Juvenile Courtroom

We return to hear the Social Services Solicitor.

SOCIAL SERVICES SOLICITOR During the adjournment I have spoken with Mr Murphy and we feel it may assist your worships to reach a decision if he were allowed to address the court further.

LADY MAGISTRATE Yes, very well.

Murphy again addressing court.

MURPHY There are men in offices in London, Mayfair, who will tonight get into their big Daimlers and go home, open their cocktail cabinets, get drunk, hit the wife or girl friend, behind high walls, in detached houses. And no one will know. I am poor. The largest loss to poverty is privacy. I go to my tiny house – it's so full of kids, their mess, their noise, I have to go out, into the public streets where I'm exposed to the public, and the police, and vulnerable. And while I tell you honestly I drink, and I've a temper that leads to violence, yet after six months since my wife died we still have a home intact, run by Maeve, and not destroyed by me. (*points to Jean*) And not, I ask you, to be destroyed by them. I will not ever go on the town again to get drunk. I will never raise my hand to Maeve again. I don't know what will be the outcome of this court but whatever happens I'm telling you I've changed. The things I did to Maeve that brought me to here are the same things that changed me. I mean that. Please, do not break up my family… (*Murphy sits down*)

The magistrates are still impressed.

36 Later

The lady magistrate waits until all are seated, addresses Jean.

LADY MAGISTRATE Inspector Darblay. (*Jean stands*) My colleagues and I have considered your application for a twenty-eight-day order and have decided, having carefully weighed the circumstances, that we are not prepared to grant it.

JEAN I'm obliged, your worships.

The magistrates stand.

COURT USHER The court will rise.

All stand.

The magistrates file out.

The various parties start to move to the exit.

Murphy in the aisle finds himself close to Jean.

MURPHY No hard feelings, Inspector.

JEAN (*to Maggie*) We lost.

Jean looks at him expressionlessly.

She moves to the exit, Tom about ten feet in front of her.

37 The anteroom of the Juvenile Court

Jean comes out.

Murphy comes up to Tom.

MURPHY Mr Darblay, how about a little drink?

The camera pauses on Tom. He's suddenly angry.

TOM (*controlled voice*) What are you talking about? What have you just told the court? You'd give up drink...

MURPHY Come on, a little victory drink.

TOM No, and don't you forget the appointment at the police station at seven o'clock tonight. The assault charges still have to be dealt with.

MURPHY (*snaps*) All right. (*Murphy, miffed, turns to Maeve*) Collect the kids. Take them home.

Murphy walks off.

Maeve looks at Tom, then moves to another exit.

Meanwhile Tom becomes aware that Jean is standing there on the opposite side of the room, looking at him. He takes a symbolic deep breath, and moves across to her.

JEAN Well?

(*Pause*)

TOM Well, we both lost.

JEAN Yes. (*A long moment while they wonder where to take the conversation from here*) It changes a lot – you and me.

TOM What does it change?

JEAN I can't count on you, a hundred percent, in the future. Count on your hundred percent support.

(*another pause*)

TOM Maybe that's a good thing.

JEAN How?

TOM To know we've both got our principles and to realise we're prepared to fight for them and not compromise them within a marriage.

JEAN Is that what *you* think?

TOM Yes.

JEAN We'll see.

They're looking at each other – they're not going to be able to sort this out here and now – there's the sense that they're not going to sort this one out ever. They did what they had to do. But it is a lesson to Jean. She had come to rely on a kind of rubber-stamp support from Tom. She can't be so sure of that in future.

Tom gives a little shrug, takes her hand.

TOM (*gently*) Come on. Lunch hour. Let's go home, it's nearly lunchtime. I'll make you an omelette.

JEAN No, I've got something else for you to do.

38   The carport alongside the Darblays' house

We see Tom, a disgusted look on his face, hosepipe in left hand, sponge in other, attempting to clean the caked custard off the Mini. The camera slowly pans to a bedroom window. There's Jean, no expression on her face, studying Tom, and then there dawns slowly a small smile at the ridiculous spectacle of Tom, cursing away, custard all over him, trying to clean the car.

Expectations

Paula Milne

The Cast

Inspector Jean Darblay

Sergeant Joseph Beck

Sergeant George Parrish

PC Roland Bentley

WPC Hannah Maynard

Tom Darblay

Jennie Randall

Vivian Maxley

Dr Jason

Laura Cartwright

Shop Manager

Counter assistant

Mo

Lax

Small boy

Jack Cartwright

Policeman

Expectations

1 The bedroom of the Darblays' house

There's just one pool of light in the room, the bedside light being the only illumination.
Except, next to the bed, we see the flicker of a black and white portable television, its volume turned down very low. Some kind of old romantic film is on.
Tom is lying in the bed, a large file of paperwork in his lap.
But he is not looking at it, nor is he looking at the television.
He is simply lying there staring at nothing.
A second later we hear Jean approach the bedroom.
Hastily Tom stuffs the file of papers out of sight, under a pillow.
Jean enters, wearing a nightdress and dressing gown. She's in the middle of washing her hair, and has a towel over her head.
She smiles at him briefly, collects a bottle of hair conditioner from her dressing table, and exits again.
As Jean closes the door, her uniform, hanging on the back of it, starts to swing gently on its hanger. It causes Tom to pause, watching it.
We can hear the sound of running water, and bathroom ablutions, perhaps the sound of Jean humming.
After a moment Tom turns rather abruptly away from the uniform, as though it is offering some kind of mute challenge he is disinclined to meet.
But almost immediately his eye strikes something else: Jean's personal radio, on the bedside table.
He reaches out and switches it on, and the room is instantly filled with static, then:
RADIO (*voice off*) Correction 7321 – the address is 94, repeat 94 Portwood Street...(*a pause, then*) Hartley to 8077... (*brief pause*) 8077 go to the Three Tuns public house, neighbours report a disturbance in the car park, quick as you can, over ... Thanks ...out.
During all of this Tom simply lies, listening.
After a moment Jean enters to stand in the doorway, watching him.

Jean's hair is damp from her bath, and she is rubbing it with a towel. She moves towards the radio.

JEAN Hey...

She switches it off, her tone is without rancour, more curiosity.

Don't I get enough of that all day?

TOM That's why we keep it by our bed all night, every night is it?

JEAN (*mildly*) You know why...because anywhere else it might get nicked...

She puts it into a drawer.

Better?

TOM (*a grudging grin*) Marginally.

She sits on the bed next to him.

They simply remain there a moment, watching the antics on the screen.

Tom yawns slightly.

JEAN Tired?

TOM A bit.

Tom puts an arm around her as they watch.

TOM I'm on duty again this weekend, did I tell you?

JEAN Oh, Tom...

TOM We've got people away on leave. I couldn't very well refuse.

JEAN It's the second weekend in a month.

TOM Nonsense.

There's a pause.

JEAN I thought we'd do something nice...take ourselves off somewhere.

TOM Jean...I warned you when I started social work, it wouldn't be a nine to five job. Besides, I don't give you a hard time when it happens to you, do I?

The point is a fair one dnd she accepts it.

JEAN No...

TOM Well then...

JEAN You don't exactly go overboard about it either.

TOM (*with a grin*) Always have to get the last word, don't you?

JEAN As a rule.

He kisses her, but the phone instantly rings, startling them both.

Both immediately sigh. Tom, with a kind of wearied resignation, Jean, because she knows the effect the phone call might have on him.

(*into telephone*) Hartley 2595...speaking...When?...Did he make any statement?

She glances over at Tom as she speaks.
He simply watches the televison, impassively.

What's the problem then?...I see...no, don't do anything now, I'll follow it up in the morning...Right. Thanks for letting me know.

She hangs up and glances at Tom once again.

TOM Bit late for shop talk isn't it?

JEAN There's been a development on that Moor Park Lane job ...I asked them to keep me posted.

He says nothing, then he gets out of bed, and abruptly turns off the television.

I was watching that...

TOM We should get some sleep.

He snaps off the light, leaving her, still wearing her dressing gown, seated on the bed.
Silently she takes it off and gets into the bed.
Then Jean catches sight of the forgotten file of paperwork under his pillow.
She glances at Tom.

JEAN Tom?

TOM What?

Something in his tone deters her.
She lies down.

JEAN Goodnight...

TOM 'Night.

We hold on both faces, turned away from each other in the darkness, inexplicably and privately troubled.

2 Outside a bus station (early morning)

We are looking at a statue of Queen Victoria outside a bus station. We can just hear the dawn chorus, and the sound of the early shift arriving. We cut to see the interior of a bus shelter. Two punk girls are lying huddled together for warmth on the bench. They are both dead asleep. Even so, we can tell they are no more than fifteen or so. They have their hair cut punk style, with perhaps a slash of colour in it somewhere. And their eyes are blackened and over made-up. Both wear anoraks, tight trousers and boots. There is a large holdall between them, suggesting they have been travelling rough for some time. We concentrate on one, Lax. Slowly she opens her eyes. And we see her point of view, the graffiti-stained statue. We hold on her for a moment, looking at the graffiti.

Then she rises, and takes out a large felt-tipped pen from a pocket, and starts to scrawl on the stone.
She is just completing the job when a shout halts her.
POLICEMAN Hey...you!
A policeman is bearing down on her fast.
Lax tugs at the sleeping girl next to her, Mo, and both girls hurriedly collect up their things and start to spring away.
The policeman reaches the bus shelter, but doesn't bother to give chase.
Instead he turns to look at the statue and the words she has written.

3 Jean's car

The camera shows us Jean driving. Tom is in the passenger seat. He is leafing through that bulging case file again. Jean glances at him, in some concern.
However, when she speaks, she manages to keep her tone light, casual.
JEAN Heavy day?
TOM You could say.
We hold on Jean's face, building to speak.
JEAN I was thinking how about you and me having lunch today?
He glances at her quickly.
JEAN Well why not? Let the world and its problems manage without us for an hour.
TOM You're in uniform.
JEAN So I'll wear a coat.
Tom says nothing. It's as if he senses that there is more behind her suggestion than she is revealing.
Jean glances quickly at him.
JEAN We could do with a break...get away from everything for a while.
Tom says nothing.
Jean, casual, her eyes on the road.
JEAN Give us a chance to talk as well.
Tom looks over at her.
TOM About what?
JEAN Tom...
She reaches for his hand.
JEAN You think I haven't seen how depressed you are lately? I want to help...if you'll give me the chance.
Tom says nothing. He simply sits, her hand in his.

TOM Call me later, when I know how the day's shaping up.

JEAN Right.

They are now at his office, and she halts the car. He packs up his papers and gets ready to go.

JEAN Tom?

Tom pauses.

JEAN Try and make it if you can?

TOM (*simply, without rancour*) If you think it'll solve anything.

He goes. We hold on her, watching in concern, as he mounts the steps to his office.

4 The social workers' office

It is an open-plan office with a few desks scattered about, and one or two very young social workers. Mostly, they are trying to do paper work and this is the only time of day they might get the chance. Altogether the atmosphere is one of organised chaos: telephones ringing, a suggestion of scurrying to look up something in filing cabinets.

Jennie Randall is seated at a desk, dialling on the telephone.

JENNIE Matron, please.

As she holds, Tom enters. She glances at him briefly.

Oh, Tom, have you done those case notes on the Brent children, yet?

TOM I'm still working on them.

JENNIE Looks like we've found foster parents for them...try and get them done by tomorrow will you?

(*the telephone calls her attention*) Yes, yes, I'm still holding.

Tom is taking off his coat.

Their dialogue is played out against the background action of the office: some to-ing and fro-ing. A messenger delivering post, someone distributing coffee in plastic cups.

TOM Any messages?

Jennie shuffling through some notes on her desk.

JENNIE You had a call from the DHSS ... querying a benefit. And a Doctor Herrick rang about that Geriatric patient again. (*The telephone calls her*) Hello, Matron? This is Miss Randall, social worker, Hartley council...(*she covers the mouth-piece and holds out some papers to Tom*) The rest are on there ...

As Jennie continues her telephone conversation, Tom takes the notes from her and moves to his desk.

He opens a diary on it, and scrawls in...'Lunch, Jean?' Almost immediately the phone rings

TOM (*into phone*) Tom Darblay.

He listens a moment, his manner noticeably altering.

He becomes tense almost, defensive.

Of course I had no idea... Yes, I'll tell her...right.

He hangs up.

JENNIE Problems?

TOM An emergency case conference's been called, on the Cartwright couple.

JENNIE You saw them yesterday, didn't you?

He doesn't reply. He seems distracted suddenly.

Didn't you?

TOM Yes...and apparently within an hour of my leaving he was setting about her. She was admitted into casualty and had ten stitches put into her head.

JENNIE What happened to her?

TOM An "accident".

JENNIE Again?!

TOM Exactly.

JENNIE Oh-er...

Tom says nothing. She glances at him.

Well there's no way you could predict it would happen, Tom...

TOM So why the conference?

JENNIE Routine...

TOM Good try, Jennie. (*He rises, collects his coat*) I'm going round there, see what I can find out. Can I borrow your car?

JENNIE (*cautiously*) Is that a good idea, do you think?

TOM I can always bus it.

He's deliberately misunderstood her and she knows it. She holds out her car keys, and he takes them. We hold on her face.

5 A corridor, by the cells in Hartley Police Station

A young girl, aged about nineteen, is walking up the corridor, glancing curiously about her.

She is wearing the uniform of a woman police constable. She's a well built, almost plump girl, with a kind of earnest confidence about her, the kind of overt confidence only youth can give you. Unclouded, as yet, by experience or self doubt.

She pauses by a notice board to look at the notices pinned on it.

Curiously, she starts to look at one, lifting it up, to see what is written on the one underneath it.

Suddenly the whole bunch of papers fall off, and scatter across the floor.

Quickly, she goes down on all fours to retrieve them. But freezes, seeing a pair of feet standing in front of her. Bentley is standing over her, a cup of tea in his hand. Quickly she scrambles, up, adjusting her uniform. Bentley hands the tea over.

HANNAH Thank you very much.

BENTLEY She won't be long now.

Hannah smiles faintly, as he prepares to walk away.

HANNAH I thought it would be larger somehow.

He pauses in his tracks.

You know . . . more happening. Is it always this quiet?

BENTLEY We get our share of the action, what there is going.

HANNAH I hope so.

And there is something disconcerting about the confident way she says it. Bentley starts to move off again.

Oh, constable?

Once again, with a kind of world weary patience, he pauses.

HANNAH No sugar next time please.

Bentley correctly deems this unworthy of a reply, and goes. Hannah is about to drink her tea, when she hears voices. Hastily she looks around for somewhere to put the tea, as Jean comes into view, with Beck.

JEAN Sounds like a pretty fair night's work, who did the arrest?

BECK Hanrahan. You want to say something to him?

They are now pausing outside Jean's office.

Hannah stands poised nearby, practically at attention.

JEAN So long as it doesn't go to his head...ask him to look in
when he comes on duty... *She is about to enter when she catches sight of Hannah.*

Hello...

HANNAH Ma'am.

BECK Er...WPC Hannah Maynard, ma'am. Just checked in.

JEAN Right. (*she moves to open the door to her office*) I won't be a
moment...

HANNAH Yes, ma'am. Thank you, ma'am.

We should feel she is seriously tempted to salute. Jean gives her a slightly amused glance, and enters her office, followed by Beck.

6 Jean's office

We watch Jean and Beck, entering.
Jean turns to look at him, with eyebrows raised in query. Beck grins and picks up a file from her desk.

BECK Temporary attachment from training school...HQ sent word about her last month.

JEAN I thought we specifically requested an experienced officer?

BECK Request was specifically denied. (*she looks at him*) They reckon we're lucky to get even her.

JEAN (*leafing briefly through the file*) Ten weeks training...marvellous, isn't it? The whole point of the exercise was to have someone experienced so I wouldn't have to drop everything every time we needed a female officer for something... (*she breaks off*) Have you talked to her yet?

Beck grins, like it's a private joke.

BECK I have.

JEAN And?

BECK And usual wide-eyed innocent, full of youthful confidence.

He grins again.

JEAN Oh lor.

BECK Right.

JEAN You'd better check the duty rota, someone'll have to take her out, show her the patch.

BECK Right...

As he moves to go, Jean picks up a telephone.

JEAN Why is it the whole idea of wide-eyed innocence and youthful confidence sounds so horribly depressing?

She starts dialling

BECK Dunno, ma'am...never experienced it.

JEAN (*smiling slightly, then speaks into the telephone*) Tom Darblay, please...

7 The social workers' office

Jennie is leaning over Tom's desk, answering the telephone.

JENNIE I'm afraid he's not here at the moment. ...Is that Jean? ...I'll tell him, yes. 'Bye.

She hastily scribbles a note and places it on his desk.
It reads: "Your wife rang..."

But within a second, the note is covered by a file, dumped on Tom's desk by a passing social worker.

8   Some council flats

Each flat has a balcony running alongside the rows of front doors.
Tom is crouching by one of the front doors, shouting through the letter box.

TOM Come, on, Laura, stop playing silly buggers, I know you're in there…

There is no response from within.

TOM Look I just want to talk, all right?

A stubborn silence greets him.

TOM You're not achieving anything. I'll be back and you know it!

Impatiently he rattles at the letter box, but with no results.
Finally, resignedly, he leaves.

9   Laura's flat

As yet, we do not see anything of the flat.
We are looking at a woman's face, pressed against a wall, listening, as Tom departs.
She is in her mid-forties, a wrung-out, bruised kind of face.
A savage cut, runs along her forehead, and down, into her cheek.
After a moment, she turns, to look at a door, which is slowly opening a few inches.
We can see a glimpse of a wheel chair, and the face of a man, staring at her.
As she looks at him, something seems to flicker across her face: a look of unmistakable apprehension.

10   Council flats area

We watch Tom, pulling the car out of the forecourt to the flats, and driving off.
But we remain, for ambling about the cars parked in the forecourt are the two punks.

They are trying to open car doors as they pass.
They just have one open when footsteps signal someone approaching, and once again, they sprint off, giggling as they go, like the whole thing is just a lark...

11 Jean's office

Jean is at her desk with Hannah sitting opposite, straight backed, hands neatly folded on her lap.
Jean is leafing through her file.

JEAN So you worked in an office originally?

HANNAH Yes, ma'am.

JEAN Doing what?

HANNAH Typing, filing. General office dogsbody. It bored me rigid.

JEAN (*a small smile*) And you decided police work wouldn't?

HANNAH I wanted to do something a little more demanding than pounding a typewriter.

That unnerving confidence is there again.
Jean turns a page of the file.

JEAN I see you specially asked for this attachment? (*She looks at Hannah*) Why here, in particular?

HANNAH (*with disconcerting frankness*) Because of you.

Jean stares at her, puzzled.

You came to the training school, gave us a talk about women's integration in the force, how it's been for the good, how women still have to try twice as hard to prove themselves, but they could do it if they had the determination...

It comes out like a set speech she's pre-rehearsed for the occasion.
Jean cuts in on it.

JEAN I obviously made an impression.

HANNAH You did.

Again, that frank confidence.
She's treating Jean as an equal, or even as if she is the one doing the interviewing.

JEAN (*mildly*) And you thought...by asking for this posting... that you'd get...preferential treatment?

Hannah wasn't expecting this, it wasn't part of the plan.

HANNAH Not at all...why d'you say that?

JEAN It's one interpretation...

Hannah regards her a moment, when she speaks her tone is defiantly defensive suddenly.

HANNAH I simply wanted to work under someone I admired and respected. Is there anything wrong with that?

JEAN That's important to you?

HANNAH Of course, isn't it to you?

Jean smiles slightly again but doesn't reply.
She's quite enjoying the interview.

JEAN And supposing I don't live up to your expectations, what then? (*The camera concentrates on Hannah's face, puzzled*).
   What I'm saying is, giving a lecture on theory is one thing, putting it into practice is another...You might not find that relaxed performance you saw me give at the training school applies here...it doesn't.

HANNAH (*defensive again*) You asked me why I applied for this attachment and I've told you the reason...

JEAN And I'm simply suggesting there might be more appropriate ones...the job is what counts, not the people who do it.

There's a pause.

HANNAH Yes, ma'am.

Her tone is now starkly formal, as if resenting the authority in Jean's tone.

JEAN I...don't get the feeling I've explained myself too well.

HANNAH Oh, I think I understand what you're saying, ma'am.

Jean regards her a moment.
They seem to have reached an impasse.

JEAN Right, well we'll talk again when you've found your feet. ... In the meantime I'll show you about and I think Sergeant Beck is going to second you to someone, so you can do a patrol duty.

HANNAH Yes, ma'am, thank you, ma'am.

Jean glances at her, reacting to the cold subservience of her tone.
She decides now is not the time to pursue it and rises, leading the way to the door.
We hold briefly on Hannah's face, before she rises to follow.

12   The desk area

Jean is pointing down the corridor.

JEAN Interview Room A...Interview Room B...(*She indicates another door*).

HANNAH ...Actually PC Bentley's already shown me where everything is...I'd just as soon start work, if it's all right with you.

JEAN (*casting her a quick look*) Perfectly.

Parrish is at the desk, talking into the telephone.

PARRISH (*into phone*) Can you describe them? (*he makes a note*) And you saw them running off where? ... Right, we'll send someone over to check it out, thank you.

He hangs up.

JEAN Trouble?

PARRISH Doubt it...An old girl spotted two lasses messing about with cars over at Castle Barnes Estate an hour ago ...only she didn't bother to report until she'd got her curlers out and come back from the launderette...they're probably half way to Manchester by now.

JEAN Well, send Bentley over there when he goes out on patrol ...

PARRISH Right...

JEAN (*with a small smile*) And er...perhaps he'd like to take Hannah with him. She's rather anxious to get started.
(*turning to Hannah*) I'll go chase him up for you.

HANNAH Thank you. ma'am.

Jean exits, and Parrish glances at Hannah, the stiff erect back, the formal pose.

PARRISH Had the old welcoming routine have you?

HANNAH (*after a beat*) Something like that.

Parrish grins slightly at her tone, and leans over, very confidential all of a sudden – light-hearted, humorous.

PARRISH Don't let first impressions mislead you, love. Under that steel facade beats a heart of solid wrought iron.

The camera rests on Hannah's face – not sure how to take him.

13 The social workers' office

Desks have been pushed together as a make-shift table. Vivian Maxley, the social worker team leader, is at the head of the table.
She's in her mid-forties, a tough, laconic woman, efficient, but tending to be brusque and to the point.
She somewhat pointedly glances at her watch, and then looks at Jennie

Randall who is seated further up the table. Others present are: Doctor
Jason (the Cartwrights' GP), the woman responsible for home helps, the
man from the Day Centre, and a note taker.
There's an impatience about the gathering, as if they're anxious to get on,
but something is delaying the proceedings.
After a moment, Tom enters, bearing a bulging case-file.

TOM Sorry...

He slides into a vacant seat.
Vivian casts him a look. She briefly consults some notes.

VIVIAN A recap...we've been supervising the Cartwrights for
    just over eighteen months, since Jack Cartwright had his
    accident and became wheel-chair bound... There's a recur-
    rent history of drink, intermittent violence, and a general
    failure to cope with their altered situation, particularly on
    the part of Mrs Cartwright... (*she breaks off*) Anything you
    want to add, Jennie?

JENNIE Tom's been dealing with this one...

VIVIAN Tom?

TOM Well...things had been improving...except yesterday
    morning I received a letter from Laura, Mrs Cartwright,
    saying things were going badly wrong again and...

VIVIAN Have you got the letter?

Tom digs about in the file, and in doing so, spills some of the papers.
There's a moment, while he retrieves them, and we take in some of the
expressions of the group, waiting.
Tom hands Vivian the letter.

TOM So...anyway, I called round there late yesterday after-
    noon, but when I went, she said it was a mistake. (*He pauses.*
    Vivian looks at him.)

VIVIAN Is that it?

TOM I pressed her about it, naturally, but she said she'd written
    the letter while depressed, but now felt much better...

A moment of silence.

VIVIAN Doctor?

GP Was the husband present at this meeting?

TOM Yes...

VIVIAN What did he have to say?

TOM (*a beat*) Nothing...

VIVIAN But you discussed this letter...the one she'd written
    ...in his presence?

TOM I did, yes.

VIVIAN Was that wise? (*We watch Tom's face, glancing around at the other faces, watching him.*) ...I understood he resents our supervision anyway...that he regards it as state interference... He can't have been too pleased when he heard she's written to you behind his back...?

TOM Look, he knew about the letter, I'm sure of it.

VIVIAN How long were you there?

TOM Ten minutes?

GP And an hour later she's on her way to hospital.

TOM So you assume my visit and what happened to her are linked?

VIVIAN We simply want to know what, if anything, you picked up at the meeting. If you sensed something wrong between them...

TOM If I had sensed something, wrong, I'd have done something about it, wouldn't I?

There's a slightly awkward silence.

JENNIE It's quite in character for Laura to write a letter like that ...a letter she doesn't really mean...her behaviour isn't exactly rational at the best of times...

VIVIAN Except she clearly did mean it, because what she was worried about, happened...

JENNIE And it would have happened with or without, a visit from us...

GP That's a matter of opinion...

JENNIE (*sharply*) Yes, well I don't think anyone should be condemned on an opinion, do you?

GP Look – she called it an accident – which is what she said last time and the time before that. What kind of accident in God's name?

Another silence, this time more embarrassed.

VIVIAN What's her condition now, Doctor?

GP (*briefly consulting some notes*) The injury itself sounds straightforward enough...I'll look in later today...check it out ...

TOM If she lets you in.

VIVIAN (*turning to him*) You've been back?

TOM Of course. As soon as I heard what had happened. What did you expect?

VIVIAN I expected you to wait. (*She turns to Jennie*) I want you to get straight round there, Jennie, assess the situation ... find out what really happened, and report back to me with appropriate recommendations. We'll reconvene at four o'clock.

Jennie glances at Tom.

JENNIE Right.

Vivian starts to stack her papers up.

VIVIAN Thanks for your time everyone.

The GP, social workers and others start to raggedly troop out.

Tom moves to his desk, and Jennie to hers.

Vivian pauses, looking at Tom.

She glances at the door, ensuring everyone has gone.

VIVIAN Tom? (*he turns to face her*) The whole purpose of this meeting is to decide what action, if any, to take.

TOM So?

VIVIAN So it's a somewhat pointless exercise if that decision is pre-empted by some one acting on their own initiative, and without consultation, wouldn't you say?

TOM You're asking my opinion, are you? Only I got the impression it wasn't rated too highly.

Vivian regards him steadily.

She then turns, effectively dismissing him, to Jennie.

VIVIAN We'll speak later.

She goes.

Jennie turns to Tom.

Tom moves, in some anger, to the window.

JENNIE (*after a moment*) Come on, Tom ... you know what Doctor Jason thinks of social workers...he regards us as... amateur do-gooders. He's virtually said as much. (*Tom says nothing. She looks at his turned back*) And you haven't got the monopoly on her reprimands either. We've all had to suffer them.

TOM It's rather different for me, isn't it?

JENNIE Why, because she's a woman?

TOM Because everyone round here seems to think I was born the day before I started this job. I wasn't. I held down a job...a very responsible job...for fifteen years! And I didn't become a social worker to be slagged off by anyone who cares to take a pot shot at me!

JENNIE You expected you'd be thanked by everyone.

TOM Why not? Just by way of a change.

There's a pause, they are confronting each other, but yet it isn't each other they are angry with.

JENNIE Look...whether you like it or not you're still in training ...and taking criticism is all part of it. It is possible... conceivable, that you *did* make a mistake... We'll just have to see when we get there.

TOM (*glancing at her*) We?

JENNIE Yes, *we*. As senior social worker on the case I can still make *some* decisions...

Tom collects his coat.

His anger is spent now, to be replaced by something else.

A nagging self doubt.

TOM What if I did...make a mistake?

JENNIE We'll have to examine how and why.

TOM Dear God, you make me sound like one of your clients. (*then, glancing at her face*) Well why not? I do the same thing with Jean...I find myself questioning everything she says and why...(*then, an abrupt change of tone*) It doesn't help. Are you right?

She looks at him puzzled. She isn't sure what to make of his last comment, or if now is the time to develop it.

14   The locker room at the police station

We find Bentley, struggling into his coat, Hannah rather impatiently waiting.

BENTLEY Sergeant Beck said to show you round the patch while we're at it...

HANNAH Fine. (*Bentley starts hunting in his pockets*) Constable? (*she rather pointedly points to the table, where the car keys are lying. Bentley picks them up.*)

BENTLEY Right then.

He moves to the door, but Hannah doesn't shift.

HANNAH Constable? (*her tone is like that of a teacher, addressing an errant school child. Bentley pauses, and turns*) Don't you need this? (*she is holding out his hat, which Bentley takes*)

BENTLEY (*pointedly*) The name's Roland. (*as she blinks at him*) When you're addressing someone of the same rank you don't stand on ceremony...or didn't they teach you that at training school? (*and quickly before she can get the last word, he exits.*)

15 The station corridor

Bentley and Hannah are making for the exit.
Hannah is pulling out a map from her bag as they go.
HANNAH Which route are we taking?
BENTLEY Whatever's the quickest.
HANNAH In that case it's the bypass. I bought an Ordnance
Survey map before I arrived...I'll navigate if you like.
Unless you prefer I drive?
There's a brief shot of Bentley's face, before they swing out of the doors.
We cut to see Jean, consulting some paperwork with Beck in the corridor.
BECK She's keen, you can't deny it.
JEAN She's that all right. I just hope he can stand the pace...

16 Part of town

Bentley is pointing to something out of the window as they pass.
BENTLEY Industrial estate ... traffic's the worst headache ... eve-
ning rush hour especially.
HANNAH We had a special course on traffic as part of our train-
ing.
BENTLEY Oh?
HANNAH Just classroom theory mainly...but they reckoned
"flexitime" would solve half of the rush problems.
BENTLEY (*unimpressed*) Did they?
HANNAH Perhaps your Inspector should have a word with some
of the employers...explain the problem traffic has on the
deployment of police manpower?
BENTLEY May be you'd like to suggest it to her?
Hannah glances at him.

17 Another part of town

The pair are now driving through a well-heeled area. Detached houses
in large, expansive gardens, expensive cars parked in the drives.
BENTLEY Moor Park Lane...a bit of your stockbroker belt...
where we get the pro break-ins...and if we've got the men
we try and do a patrol most nights...made an arrest last
night as a matter of fact...from a job last Easter...

HANNAH You did?

BENTLEY One of the night lads.

HANNAH I've not done an arrest yet...have you?

Bentley smiles to himself.

BENTLEY One or two.

HANNAH Mind you, we covered most of it in training, the pro-
cedures and so forth. But I dare say there's a lot more to
it than that...it would be naive to think otherwise.

BENTLEY (*after a beat*) Just a touch.

18 · The camera cuts to the council flats

*The police car is driving into the forecourt. The car stops. Hannah
immediately gets out.*

BENTLEY They'll be well away by now, the report was an hour
old when we got it.

HANNAH We can talk to the witness, can't we? Come on...

And she tramps purposefully off.

Bentley reluctantly gets out of the car to follow.

We pan to see Laura's flat, and the balcony running alongside it.

*We can just discern the two figures of Tom and Jennie outside Laura's
door.*

The camera focuses on Laura who is putting out a milk bottle on the step.

She looks up, to see Tom and Jennie standing above her.

JENNIE Hello, Laura...

19 The sitting room of Laura's flat

*We have a chance now to see the flat properly. It is plainly furnished, the
wallpaper just post-war. The atmosphere is arid and neglected. We take
in food-stained plates littering the table, bottles lining the mantlepiece.*

Laura is lighting a cigarette.

Tom and Jennie stand watching her.

JENNIE Where is he?

Laura gestures towards a door.

Jennie and Tom move to it, and open it a few inches.

On a bed inside lies the man we saw earlier.

Asleep, fully clothed, mouth gaping open.

A bottle of whisky is on the table by the bed.

Jennie and Tom look briefly, before closing the door.

JENNIE Would you rather talk here, or...?

LAURA (*drearily, lifelessly*) Talk about what?

JENNIE We could start with that gash in your head.

LAURA (*flatly*) I walked into a door.

JENNIE Terrific. Now we've had the official version, how about the unofficial one?

Laura looks at Tom, and there's a sourness, a bitterness almost in the way she does it.

LAURA Ask him.

JENNIE I'm asking you. Come on, Laura... was he mad because you'd written to Tom, was that what set him off?

LAURA He knew I'd written...Christ, he should have, he only dictated the bloody letter.

Jennie looks at Tom, who grins at her triumphantly.

JENNIE Well within minutes of Tom leaving here last night, he was laying into you again. So if it wasn't Tom's visit that set him off, what was it?

LAURA I didn't say it wasn't Tom's visit.

JENNIE (*after a pause*) Do you want to explain that?

LAURA (*tonelessly*) What's the point...?

TOM Look, would it make it easier if I left?

LAURA You can do what the hell you like.

The deliberate indifference with which she says this is both insulting and disconcerting.

JENNIE I'm waiting, Laura...

LAURA ...We wrote that letter because we knew things were getting bad again...Jack was drinking again...we were fighting again... But we just didn't know how to stop it. And "he" ...(*once again, that insulting note*) said, when we felt that way, to let him know, and he'd be here...

TOM And when I asked you about it, you said it was all a mistake, remember?

LAURA (*bluntly*) It was...(*she moves, agitatedly about the room*) as soon as you walked in we knew it was. "I've only got a minute", he says..."What's the problem?", he says..."I'm on my way to another client", he says. Client! You'd think he was a bloody salesman!

JENNIE He did come as soon as he got your letter...

LAURA Oh sure...he came. He always comes. For five minutes. Ten, if you're lucky. But he always comes, oh yes.

TOM I do have other people on my list you know, Laura...

LAURA People? Is that what you call them? I thought they were just names and numbers...

TOM ...Oh come on, you know I don't operate like that.

LAURA Oh? (*and once again, her tone is insulting, hostile*)

JENNIE I don't get any of this, Laura...when Tom took over your case, you were really pleased...

LAURA Then he didn't just give advice did he? He gave a bit of time, to go with it...(*she looks at Tom again*) D'you know what he does when he comes here? Before ringing the doorbell? He stands there, outside, looking through our file...so he can remember our names and why he's come...so he's got it all word perfect before he comes in.

Jennie looks at Tom

TOM If I do it, it's only so I'm fully acquainted with all the facts...

LAURA God, he even sounds like a bloody text book!

JENNIE Yes, well none of this explains what happened here last night.

Laura lights another cigarette and moves to sit down.

LAURA We sat in all day...waiting for him...we thought, if we could just hold out long enough, we'll be all right...we'll be able to talk it through with him. But when he came, we knew it was useless...useless.

JENNIE What was it you wanted to talk through with him? (*She doesn't reply.*) Well, it must have been something, Laura.

Another pause. Laura's agitation has increased, as if they have now come to the point of the meeting, but she can't – or won't – admit what it is.

LAURA What the hell does it matter now anyway?

TOM (*moving towards her*) It matters to me, Laura. All right, so somehow things have got fouled up between us. But that doesn't mean I don't care about you. Or that I don't want to help you.

LAURA Help! (*she rounds on him, suddenly allowing the anger to be unleashed. So suddenly, that he almost recoils away from her*) You're not around to help are you? Where are you when he starts on and on about his accident? About what it's done to him, about how he isn't a man any more! Every night, the same thing, over and over! Eh? Where are you? (*She steps angrily up to him, pointing to her scar.*) You want to know how I got this? He hit me. With a bottle. And I

let him do it. Just like I always do. (*bitterly*) And you talk
to me about help!

TOM But why?...*Why* d'you let him do it?

LAURA (*shouting the words out at him, as if defying him to challenge
them*) Because he has to lash out at someone, doesn't he?
Hurt someone! And if I don't let him do it to me...

*She breaks off abruptly, as if she's said more than she intended to. She
starts to turn away from him, but he catches her arm, and pulls her to
face him.*

TOM If you don't let him do it to you, what...? (*She says nothing.*)
What, Laura?

LAURA (*angrily almost spitting the words out at him*) I'm afraid he'll
end up doing something to himself! (*then her distress mounting*) Now get out! You've got what you came for...go and
write it up in one of your files, but get out.

(*Helplessly she starts to strike at his chest, flailing and pummelling at
him*) Get out...!

*And as Tom catches her and restrains her, she slumps against him, weep-
ing.*

Jennie and Tom exchange a look over her head.

20 Outside the flat

*We watch Tom leaving the flat. He moves to stand at the balcony, bleakly
looking at the urban landscape about him, the effect of the previous conversation is very evident in his face.*

*We move, to see the police car pulling out of the parking lot, and cut to
the interior of the car.*

BENTLEY I told you, they'll be well clear by now.

HANNAH (*consulting her map again*) It was worth a try... Now then,
how about seeing some of the town itself? We can go north
up Canal Street...left into Junction Road and then fork
right into the top of the High Street...

Bentley wearily puts the car into gear, and they drive off...

21 A shopping street

*The camera is scanning a modest shopping precinct. There are a few
shoppers, scattered about their business.*

We pick out Mo and Lax kicking a tin can about, laughing and yelling to each other, as they send it hurtling amongst the startled shoppers, and skidding over the pavement.

22 Social workers' office

Tom is broodily standing over his desk.
A moment later Jennie enters, and takes off her coat.
Tom glances at her.

TOM Well?

JENNIE I suggested we send a psychiatrist around...we'll just have to see what he recommends and take it from there. (*he says nothing, she glances at him*) Tom, why on earth didn't you tell me things were going so badly wrong?

TOM (*simply*) I didn't think they were.

JENNIE How many cases have you got on at the moment?

TOM Off hand...God knows.

JENNIE Approximately?

TOM Forty...

JENNIE Forty! How?

TOM Some are follow ups from my intake duties...referrals, we've got two people away on leave, I offered to supervise some of their cases while they're...

JENNIE ...You're supposed to check with *me* before you take on new cases...

TOM I thought I could handle it.

JENNIE It's too much, Tom.

TOM So what am I supposed to do? Hand them back and say I can't cope?

JENNIE That's exactly what you're supposed to do. What do you think? People are going to say you've failed because you can't take on a new case? It doesn't work like that, Tom. I told you, from the word go...pace yourself.

TOM I wanted to prove I was up to it.

JENNIE Why? We're not in competition with each other... It's not a job you can measure success in like that!

TOM (*angrily*) All right then... I'll elbow half my case load!

JENNIE Tom, I'm *trying* to work out what's gone wrong! (*there's a moment of angry silence between them. Jennie sits down, almost defeatedly*) It's probably my fault. I could see you were...

(*she pauses*) I should have said something before... I just assumed it had something to do with Jean.

Tom looks at her sharply.

TOM Jean? Why?

JENNIE I don't know. Things you've said. Or rather haven't said.

TOM Do us a favour will you, Jennie? Save the psychoanalysis bit for the clients?

He walks out.

We hold on her face.

The camera follows Tom's face as he bangs out of the office, revealing not just anger, but a kind of remorse for his words.

She has clearly touched a nerve.

23 The shopping centre

Bentley and Hannah are now in the town.

Suddenly, Hannah speaks, so suddenly, it takes him by surprise.

HANNAH Stop the car.

Bentley abruptly draws the car to a halt.

BENTLEY What is it?

HANNAH I want to do walkabout.

BENTLEY Eh?

Hannah folds up her map as she speaks.

HANNAH The training school said that if you want to get to know a place and the people in it, there's no better way than getting out there amongst them.

BENTLEY We're *supposed* to stick together...

Hannah now has the car door open.

HANNAH We're also supposed to use our initiative, right? I'll only be half an hour...

BENTLEY Well make sure you are. I'll meet you here in thirty minutes! Be here!

She waves airily to him, and continues walking off.

He looks after her, worried by her decision, yet immensely relieved to be shot of her for a while.

Hannah watches as the police car pulls away from her.

She then turns, to look up the street.

Rather self consciously, she adjusts her jacket, and starts to walk, very straight-backed, down the road.

But then pauses – in a shop window she can see her reflection.

She's obviously not seen herself like that before, "in situ" as it were, and in uniform.
The sight seems to impress her. Chin held up high, she continues her patrol down the street.

24 A departmental chemist store

The camera wanders into a large departmental chemist store. We see the two punks, trying on pairs of sun glasses – giggling and laughing – causing the rotating display to spin wildly and the contents to fly off.
They move on to another counter where items of make-up are displayed.
They pause long enough to scoop various bits of merchandise into their hold-all and pockets, before ambling on.
We cut, to see they are being observed, by the manager of the store.
The two girls are now beside another counter, and the manager covertly signals to a counter assistant, who moves to join him.
Once again, the girls are briskly filling their pockets. Then, as if sensing they are being observed, they start to head for the exit.
Immediately the manager and the counter assistant follow, at a distance. The girls walk straight past the pay booth, and out of the shop.
We watch, through the shop window, as the girls move out of the doors – but their departure is abruptly curtailed by the manager and counter assistant who stop them and lead them, protesting, back towards the store. And we, like the few gaping shoppers, watch the incident, like a mute pantomine.
The camera returns to Hannah, in a wide shot. She's got her map out again and is attempting to direct a passerby. She then continues her patrol, still with that confident, rather proud gait.
She pauses, a small boy is following her.
She turns and he grins at her, uttering the single phrase:
Hoink hoink…*before his mother quickly yanks him off.*
Hannah is about to move on, when suddenly the manager of the chemist store darts out, and catches her by the arm.
MANAGER I need you.
We watch Hannah's face, slightly startled as she is led through the store by the Manager.

25 The manager's office

The room is an office-cum-stock room with crates and boxes piled up in a corner.
The two punk girls are seated near a desk.
The counter assistant is standing over them.
Hannah enters, with the manager.

MANAGER (*to counter assistant*) You'd better get back to your counter.

ASSISTANT Right.

He exits.

Hannah glances at the two girls, who simply sit, hands dug into pockets, watching her dispassionately.

Hannah squares herself up slightly, and addresses the Manager.

HANNAH ... Perhaps you would like to tell me what happened?

MANAGER Well, together with Mr Bailey, my counter assistant, I watched these two girls taking various items and putting them into their pockets and that bag. (*The Manager gestures to a bag lying on the desk*) It's all here... two pairs of sunglasses...a bottle of hairspray...mascara...two packs of eyeshadow...one of face cream...four pairs of tights...(*as he speaks he turns the items over on the desk for Hannah to see*) They then left the shop without making any attempt to pay. We followed them, and picked them up outside in the usual way...

Hannah now has a notebook out.

Some of her confidence seems to have ebbed slightly. She turns to face the two girls and clears her throat slightly.

HANNAH Well, you've heard what this man has said... I must warn you that you are not obliged to say anything unless you wish to, and that anything you say may be put into writing and given in evidence. (*They simply stare at her expressionlessly*) D'you understand?

Still the girls say nothing. It's as if the whole incident, including Hannah's last words, have failed to have any discernible impact on them.

HANNAH Haven't you got anything to say for yourselves at all?

LAX Yes, Miss, we didn't do it, Miss, honest we didn't.

(*and she says it tauntingly, derisively*)

Mo snorts quietly like a pig.

MANAGER Comedians, but still the same old joke.

HANNAH (*to the girls*) Very well, I'll have your names and addresses please. (*she stands, a pencil poised over her notebook.*

115

The girls simply sit, without moving) All right, we'll do it the hard way.

She moves over, and dips into their pockets, removing a wallet and purse. While she is doing this, the counter assistant puts his head round the door to address the Manager.

COUNTER ASSISTANT That dry food delivery's arrived...you said you wanted to check it before he went...

MANAGER Tell him I'll be out in a minute.

COUNTER ASSISTANT He's already unloaded, he wants to be on his way...

MANAGER *(to Hannah)* Look, I have to go... I'll throw the lock after me... Just shout if you need anything...

HANNAH Right...

MANAGER I won't be long.

He goes. Hannah glances rather nervously at the two girls and moves to the telephone.

She consults her notebook briefly, for the station number, and dials.

While she is doing this, Lax rises, almost casually from her seat.

HANNAH Would you remain seated, please? *(Lax merely looks at her, with a kind of quizzical insolence. Hannah speaks into the telephone)* Er...this is WPC Maynard...I'm at Lawsons the chemist, and I need transport back to the station for two... *(Lax takes a step towards her. Breaking off)* I said, sit down...

LAX Look at it...the original Miss Piggy...

And before Hannah can move, Lax springs on to her, wrenching the phone from her hands.

Mo immediately joins her, and both girls start to flail and punch at the struggling Hannah.

We cut to the desk area at the Police Station and find Parrish on the telephone. We can hear the muffled sound of the struggle.

PARRISH Hello? ...*(more urgently)* Hello...! *(he swings around and switches on the radio)* Hartley to 7189.

26 The police car

The car is now parked in an alley, or small street, off the high street. Bentley is at the wheel, tucking into a packet of fruit gums, and keeping an eye out for Hannah.

His radio alerts him.

PARRISH *(voice distorted)* 7189, are you there?

BENTLEY 7189 to Hartley.

PARRISH (*voice distorted*) Get yourself to Lawsons Chemist, quick as you can. WPC Maynard needs back up.

BENTLEY Right...

Spilling his wine gums in his haste, he quickly starts up the car and attempts to turn it around in the small alley. However his attempt isn't successful, and he quickly abandons any further effort, gets out and sprints off.

27 The desk area at the station

Jean has now joined Parrish.
She is pulling on her coat.

JEAN What on earth was she doing there on her own?

PARRISH Ask Bentley.

JEAN (*as she hurries out*) I intend to...and ring the manager, see if you can find out what's happening...!

She goes. Parrish turns back to the telephone.

28 Outside the stock room

We watch Bentley, with the Manager, who quickly unlocks the door. They enter to see Hannah slumped on the ground, struggling to get up.
Her nose is bloodied and her uniform torn and dishevelled. On her forehead, scored across it in black felt-tipped pen is the one word 'PIG'

BENTLEY Bloody hell...

HANNAH The fire escape...

Quickly he springs to the window and clambers out.
The manager moves to help Hannah up.

29 The back of the chemist's store

Bentley clambers out of the window, in time to catch sight of the two girls, distantly sprinting off.
He grapples for his radio.

BENTLEY Suspects – two girls – got away through a back door...am in pursuit.

He hurtles off after them.
We cut to Jean's car.
Jean is at the wheel .

We catch Parrish's message on her radio.

PARRISH ...running away from the back of Lawson's store, ma'am...

JEAN (*reaching for her radio*) I'll try and cut them off round the back.

We cut to waste ground at the rear of the shops.
The two girls can be seen running and scrambling over the waste ground.
They spot Bentley and spin round to run off in opposite direction.
Jean's car appears, bearing down on two girls.
Jean scrambles out of her car and tries to cut them off. Bentley and Jean eventually manage to corner them. They struggle.

30 Outside the chemist's store

Jean can be seen pushing through the entrance of the shop – to pull up and stare.
Hannah is threading her way through the store towards them. Her face is still bloodied, her uniform still torn and dishevelled.
That word still emblazoned across her forehead.
But she walks with that same proud confidence as before, her head held up.
And Jean, like Bentley and the gaping shoppers, simply stands, watching, as Hannah moves out of the store.

JEAN Hannah, are you all right?

31 The bedroom of the Darblays' house

The curtains are drawn, a glimmer of light half heartedly seeps through them.
The bed is unmade and rumpled.
We hear the bang of a front door and Tom's footsteps on the stairs.
He enters the bedroom and pauses, then moves, to draw back the curtains.
He starts to make the bed, but disinterestedly, like a man just going through the motions.
Something catches his attention by the bed.
It's a book, clearly marked "All about social work".
He sits down, the book in his hand, idly flipping through it a moment, before snapping it shut.
And the way he does it is like a mute rejection.

32 The corridor outside Jean's office

We watch Beck coming along the corridor, perhaps studying a clipboard as he goes.
Jean's office door is very slightly ajar, and the sound of her voice makes him pause.
JEAN (*angrily*) What on earth made you *do* it?
Beck winces slightly at her tone, and continues on his way.

33 Jean's office

Jean is angrily confronting Bentley, who stands stiffly in front of her.
JEAN I'm waiting for an explanation.
BENTLEY She insisted, ma'am.
JEAN I see! Even though you're the more experienced officer, even though she was *specifically* put in your charge, under your responsibility, she insisted on going off alone and you went along with it!
BENTLEY The idea was it would only take a minute or two, Ma'am...
JEAN In other words no one would have been any the wiser?
There's a moment of silence. Bentley doesn't quite know how to answer that one, so he just shifts his weight instead.
You do realise, that if you'd gone by the book, followed Sergeant Beck's instructions to stick with her, that none of this would have happened? That little penny has dropped I take it?
BENTLEY Yes, ma'am. (*then awkwardly*) I'm sorry, Ma'am.
JEAN (*tersely*) Unfortunately that doesn't put anything right, does it?
She exits.
Bentley exhales gently.

34 The locker room of the station

Hannah is washing at a small sink, standing in her shirt sleeves, her uniform jacket slung over a chair nearby. The word 'PIG' is still on her forehead.
After a second Jean enters, closes the door and leans against it.
Hannah rather nervously glances at her in the mirror.

JEAN Right. Now let's have your version.

HANNAH Ma'am?

JEAN (*hard*) Straight out of training school or not, Hannah, you do know you shouldn't go it alone, don't you?

HANNAH I was just looking around…

JEAN (*cutting in*) That doesn't answer my question. What exactly happened in there? With the two girls?

HANNAH They jumped me. I wasn't ready for it.

JEAN Which is why we didn't want you wandering off alone in the first place. Perhaps now that message has sunk in?

HANNAH (*in that stiff, resentful tone again*) Yes, Ma'am.

Jean regards her a moment

JEAN How about that big exit. What was all that in aid of? Couldn't you have cleaned up first?

HANNAH (*evenly*) I could have, yes.

JEAN Well?

HANNAH I thought people should know. (*Jean stares at her puzzled*) All they ever see is the other side, isn't it? The efficient, public face. I wanted them to see the other one…we have to face it every day, why shouldn't they for once?

Jean is unsure what she is getting at.

JEAN Face what exactly?

Hannah looks at her in the mirror, and then points to the word on her forehead.

HANNAH This.

JEAN Rather a melodramatic way of proving a point.

HANNAH It's the way a lot of them think of us, isn't it? What I've got to carry about with me for the rest of my working life. Perhaps I just wanted to get used to the idea!

There's a kind of aggressiveness about the way she says it, a defiance, as if it's masking something else: a confusion and doubt she's not yet worked through.

JEAN And have you?

HANNAH No.

JEAN Well whatever your reasons, I don't want to see you doing it again. Understood? If people want to think that about us, no amount of dramatic little gestures will make them change their mind. That's something you're just going to have to accept.

Hannah says nothing, she continues washing.

JEAN (*pointedly*) You can't do the job if you don't, Hannah.

Hannah glances at her.
There's a moment of silence between them.
Hannah then starts to wash the word off her forehead.
Jean watches a second, then steps towards her.

    Let me help you.

Hannah, almost reluctantly, surrenders the cloth, and Jean starts to wipe at the word on her face. Hannah raises her eyes, and the two women look at one another, as if Jean's words, and the implication behind them, have helped her reach some kind of tentative understanding.

35 The bedroom of the Darblay house

We find Jean in bed, simply lying there, like Tom before her at the start of the episode, deep in thought.
A moment later he enters, dressed for bed.

TOM I've locked up.

She smiles briefly in acknowledgement.

He moves to a cupboard, starts sorting through some clothes for the next day.

JEAN Tom? (*He breaks off, and glances at her.*) I'm still waiting to hear what happened to our lunch… (*He shuts his eyes, he's obviously forgotten all about it.*)

JEAN (*continues wryly*) So much for making time for each other.

TOM (*looking directly at her*) We've got time now, haven't we? (*she nods, and he moves over, to sit on the edge of the bed taking her hand*) So…if we'd had this lunch…what would we have talked about?

JEAN I told you… Us.

TOM And?

JEAN (*pausing a second before speaking*) How we seem to be pulling in different directions… How we never confide in each other any more… How you seem to resent it whenever I talk about work. (*She glances at him.*) Things like that.

TOM And what conclusions would we have come to?

Once again, Jean hesitates.

As if they are now getting very near to home, but Jean's suddenly reluctant to risk talking about it. Then she knows she must.

JEAN … That if we didn't want to risk our marriage…we'd have to do something about it. (*He says nothing.*) Assuming you think we are risking it?

TOM (*quietly*) Yes.

JEAN That's one thing we agree on. (*But she says it almost ruefully, as if she's been hoping he would contradict her*) Why didn't you really meet me today, Tom?

TOM I've screwed up at work, Jean.

JEAN (*after a beat*) Badly?

TOM.Bad enough.

JEAN How...why?

TOM Usual story. I took on too much, too early. (*He gets on the bed beside her, and leans against the pillows.*) When I first went into social work they gave us this little pep talk, about how you should always let your feelings guide you...when you meet a client, you tap your own feelings about them in order to understand them better. (*We see her face, quietly listening.*) Even if you feel...disgust or...you can use it constructively, because even a negative feeling is a starting point... Providing, of course, you trust your feelings, that you haven't lost the knack of feeling anything in the first place. (*She glances at him quickly, as he continues.*) Anyway... I decided all that was so much guff... Logic was what was needed. So I went for the practical approach... And I took on more and more cases just to prove I was right. (*He pauses.*) Instead of which I managed to prove I was incompetent, and irresponsible. So, after three months, I'm back where I started. My way didn't work, and, if I want to stick at it, I have to try theirs.

JEAN What's wrong with that?

TOM Nothing. Assuming I'm capable of it.

JEAN Of course you are...

TOM Except it gets to be a habit, putting a dampener on your feelings... I'm not sure I can break it. (*like a deliberate afterthought*) God knows I've been doing it with you long enough.

JEAN Me...?

TOM (*reluctantly*) You're right, about the resentment. I resent it all...the fact that when the phone rings it's never for me...that when we go out, it's always your career, which is the sole topic of conversation. (*then*) Just that everyone regards you as more successful.

JEAN But I'm not...

TOM Other people think you are.

JEAN Other people!

TOM You can't just ignore other people Jean... I care about what people think of me...

JEAN This is ridiculous, Tom…you're just trying to find a reason because your job hasn't gone as smoothly as you expected, so you're blaming mine!

TOM I'm blaming myself. If I can…just face some of the doubts I sometimes have about us…maybe I can do the same with other people.

JEAN Your clients, you mean?

TOM Yes…

JEAN So I'm to be a guinea pig for them?

TOM Look, I'm the one who's on trial. (*He looks at her, as if trying to assess the effect of his words.*) I think maybe part of what's been going wrong between us…is the same problem I have at work. Because I'm ashamed of some of the things that I feel, I've tried to ignore them. But if I'm ever going to do the job properly, if we're ever going to get back to where we were, I've got to face a few things, that's all I'm saying…

Jean turns to look at Tom directly.

JEAN That phone might ring at any moment, Tom… Are you still going to resent it?

TOM Possibly. But at least we put a name to it, right?

She says nothing for a moment, but returns to sit on the edge of the bed.

JEAN How can you resent someone you love…even if they are successful?

TOM Perhaps because you're afraid they might not love you if you're not.

Jean looks at him.

JEAN You idiot.

She moves over and kisses him.

TOM (*with a grin*) Are we ever going to get into this bed or what.

JEAN I'm on my way.

TOM Turn the box on before you do.

JEAN I thought you wanted an early night?

TOM I do. There's a fight on. *She switches the television on, and we see a match start. Then she gets into the bed next to him.*

His eyes are on the screen. You haven't told me about your day.

She opens her mouth, but thinks better of it. Perhaps instinctively realising now is not the time to open that can of beans.

JEAN Nothing to tell…

They settle down in front of the televison.

Relief

Ian Kennedy Martin

The Cast

Inspector Jean Darblay

Tom Darblay

Sergeant Joseph Beck

Sergeant George Parrish

PC Roland Bentley

PC Ian Shelton

Superintendent Lake

Inspector Robins

Sergeant Walters

Sergeant Joel

Jack Richards

Harry Richards

Mrs Creggan

Relief

1 Jean's office, Hartley Police Station

Jean is sitting at her desk gathering a hefty pile of papers together. We watch her put the papers in a wire basket which she pushes to the front of the desk. She then stands, picks up a briefcase, opens a desk drawer, takes out a pair of "uniform" court shoes and three pairs of tights in plastic wrappers, and stuffs them in the briefcase. She hesitates, mentally checking she's done everything, tidies the desk top paperweight, pen tray, photo of Tom. Everything is put in the desk drawer. She leaves on the desk a second wire filing basket which contains a few papers and memos. Gathering the first filing basket in her arms, and carrying the briefcase, together with her handbag over her shoulder, she leaves the office.

2 The desk area, Hartley Police Station

Beck is standing, writing notes on a clipboard, as Jean enters and puts the filing basket on the counter. Beck looks up and smiles.

BECK Ready for off then, ma'am?

JEAN (*indicating the filing basket*) Most of this lot's for forwarding. I've put notes on one or two that I'm not happy about. Will you see they're fixed up? I don't think there's anything else, is there?

BECK Nothing we can't deal with. You going away?

JEAN A week at home. Lazy weekend, then I'm going to try my hand at decorating, would you believe.

BECK Good luck and you'll need it, ma'am.

JEAN Now are you listening to this, Joseph?

BECK Ma'am?

JEAN You will phone me only in the direst emergency. Short of that, I don't want to hear from you, from anyone, in any way, about any matter connected with this wonderful police station. Clear?

BECK Yes, ma'am. You speaking at the Law Society dinner Wednesday?

JEAN I've got to get that speech together as well. See you Monday week. Don't any of you get into mischief while I'm away. (*she starts to leave, then turns*) Joseph, you're on nights next week?

BECK Yes, ma'am.

JEAN (*indicating basket*) There's a note for you. Young Shelton: you know his wife's expecting. They've arranged for her mother to come and stay, but she can't make it until Wednesday or Thursday. The note explains it all, but I've approved that he should work Three Area nights. See that that's fixed.

BECK Yes, ma'am.

JEAN Cheers then.

BECK Have a good leave, ma'am – we'll look after the shop while you're away. No problems.

Exit Jean.

Beck moves to the filing basket and starts sorting the papers.

3 Superintendent Lake's office

The camera shows us Lake behind a mountain of papers, mainly the weekend's reports/files, on his desk.

LAKE Come!

He goes on reading and initialling the reports as Inspector Robins enters. He's in his early thirties, aggressively well turned out: full uniform, wearing hat and gloves. Robins marches to the front of desk and stands rigidly to attention.

ROBINS Inspector Robins, Sir!

LAKE (*looking up unimpressed*) Yes, son, welcome to Division.

(*He offers a handshake without standing. They shake hands, Robins resumes his erect stance. Lake is still looking at papers*) Take off your hat, sit down. We don't stand on ceremony here. I think you'll find it a bit different from Police College. (*Robins sits on edge of a nearby chair but does not relax. Lake sits back, studying Robins*) You're a week with us before you go off to this staff job...that right?

ROBINS Yes sir.

LAKE Well, I shan't be giving you a shift of your own. You'll act as relief. That way you'll give as many of the lads as possible the benefit of your experience.

It's plain Lake's clear in his own mind where the experience is most needed.

ROBINS (*unaware of Lake's implications*) I'd be delighted to act in a relief capacity. Quite interesting to take over an established regiment for a week, sir.

LAKE I want you to cover Hartley, the usual Inspector, Inspector Darblay, is on leave. It's a twenty-four-hour cover station for the Inspector, so there are no shifts involved. Know where Hartley is?

ROBINS Driven through it a couple of times, years ago.

LAKE You can start now – if there are any problems, give me a ring.

ROBINS That won't be necessary, sir.

LAKE Whether you think it's necessary, I wish to be kept informed about my sub-division. I expect to rely on my inspectors for that.

ROBINS Of course, sir.

LAKE All right. Good luck. Carry on. I'll see you later.

ROBINS Thank you, sir.

Lake returns to his papers, ignoring Robins as he gets up and leaves. After he has gone Lake sits back, looks towards the door Robins left through and draws on his pipe thoughtfully.

4 The Darblays' house, Jean's front room

The furniture has been stacked in the centre of the room and covered with dust sheets and newspapers. A pair of steps is beside one wall and paint tins, roller and tray are on the table. Jean surveys the scene, deciding where to start as Tom enters from the hall putting on his anorak.

TOM Right, love, I'm off. See you about six.

JEAN It will be six? Phone me if you think it's going to be later. Then I won't stop to make dinner.

TOM Well don't overdo it, love – remember it is supposed to be your week off. (*They embrace briefly, an affectionate kiss.*) See you later.

After he's left, Jean picks up a tin of paint, reads the instructions and puts it down. She picks up another tin, reads the instructions and puts that down. She stands looking at her "decorating kit". Then she makes a decision: starts to open a tin, when the phone rings in the hall. Jean exits to the hall and answers the phone.

JEAN Hello – oh hello, Mrs Maudsley…

5 Jean's hall

JEAN Yes, that's right. I'm having a few days off... Meals on wheels? Yes, of course I remember. That's right. I did offer the use of my car if you were stuck...Tomorrow morning. And Wednesday. And Friday. (*her expression says "Oh no"*) But not Friday. (*grim*) Yes, I'll be glad to help out. No it's quite all right, I've got nothing arranged. (*looking at tins of paint*) Fine then, I'll call round for you at half past eleven tomorrow morning. Don't mention it, I'm sure it'll be nice to get out of the house.

She replaces the phone and goes back to the front room.

6 The desk area, Hartley Police Station

Parrish is alone in the room, behind the desk, speaking on the telephone.

PARRISH Yes, right, Charlie, Tuesday next then, eight o'clock, that's fine. Yeah, look – don't bring that Welsh git pal of yours. I know he's your right arm. (*Inspector Robins has entered suddenly and is standing there watching Parrish, who is leaning in an untidy sprawl against the duty desk, back to him, blathering away on the telephone*) But if he can't hold his drink then bloody keep him away from it. How can I play snooker if I feel that at any moment he's going to throw up all over the baize?

ROBINS (*white-faced with anger*) You!

Parrish turns, gulps at the fury on the face of the immaculately turned-out inspector.

PARRISH Sir!

ROBINS Terminate your call.

PARRISH Yes, sir. (*into telephone*) I have to go, Charlie.

Promptly replaces telephone.

ROBINS I am relief Inspector Robins.

PARRISH We've been expecting you, sir.

ROBINS Name?

PARRISH Sergeant Parrish.

Long pause.

ROBINS That wasn't the truth, was it, Sergeant Parrish? You were not expecting me. If you were, you would not have been using a police phone for what was clearly a private and disgusting conversation. So you are a liar, Sergeant, is that clear?

PARRISH Yes, sir.

ROBINS Show me the Inspector's office.

PARRISH At once, sir. Yes, sir.

Parrish, in a panic, comes fast round the desk to lead the way. Robins follows him off down the corridor.

7 Jean's office

Parrish enters and holds the door open for Robins. He comes in.

ROBINS Wait.

PARRISH Yes, sir. (*Robins moves round behind the desk, still hatted, puts his gloves in the desk, sits down and starts sorting through the papers in the filing basket.*) Er, that's Inspector Darblay's basket, sir.

ROBINS (*looks up with a withering gaze*) So I imagine, Sergeant. I've been posted here in the absence of your regular Inspector. I'm in charge for the next week and I'm not impressed with what I've seen of you so far – to whom were you speaking on the phone?

PARRISH (*confused*) I was just fixing up a snooker match with the ambulance drivers. We have a pretty close relationship on a small patch like this, sir.

ROBINS Off-duty calls are not made in a working police station. Convey that to the rest of the staff.

PARRISH Yes, sir.

ROBINS I want to see the Parade State and the allocation of beats and areas at least half an hour before each parade. Let me have a map of the area with all the beats and car areas marked on it. (*He picks up an ashtray and holds it up for Parrish to take.*) No smoking by staff anywhere in the police station in the public view. Pass that instruction to *all* staff. You may go. Send in the correspondence for my signature. (*Parrish moves out of the room without response.*) Sergeant Parrish!

Parrish is suddenly back in the room.

PARRISH (*worried*) Yes sir?

ROBINS When I give an order – "Send in the correspondence for my signature" – I expect a response – "Yes sir" or "No sir". Now, which is it?

PARRISH Yes, sir.

ROBINS Good. You may go.

PARRISH Yes, sir.

He exits. The camera focusses on Robins face. The expression there conveys the thought that if Parrish is an example of the state of affairs at Hartley, then he's going to be knocking a few heads together in the next seven days.

8   Jean's front room

Jean is ladling emulsion paint into the roller pan. She takes the roller and rolls paint onto it, climbs up and places the roller against the wall.
The front doorbell rings. Jean, a curse under her breath, turns, puts her roller back into the tray, and heads for the front door.

9   Outside the Darblays' house

Mrs Creggan, the next-door neighbour, is standing half way down Jean's path. She is a busy little woman, aged about fifty, five-foot-one in height, always on the go and talks as fast as she operates.
Jean opens the front door.

JEAN Hello, Mrs Creggan.

MRS CREGGAN Can you help me put ladder up, love? Won't take a minute of your time. Your fault. My Jack, when he heard that you were painting your house, he said, make yourself useful like Mrs Darblay next door and find out what's clogging up down pipe – it's been flooding the wall.

JEAN Right, Mrs Creggan. Lead the way.

MRS CREGGAN Thanks love.

Jean follows the hurried footsteps of Mrs Creggan, out of the front gate, in through the next door front gate, up the path and round the side of the semi, towards the back.

MRS CREGGAN How's progress, love?

JEAN (*grim*) Haven't really had a chance to get started yet, love.

MRS CREGGAN What paint did you buy, love? Is it that plastic stuff? Is it thixotropic?

JEAN I think so.

MRS CREGGAN You've made a mistake there. When you come to wash it, it peels off like bird droppings. It's this way, love. Have you done your dead ends yet?

10 The back of Mrs Creggan's house

We watch Mrs Creggan arrive and fetch the ladder out of the shed.

MRS CREGGAN (*indicating the ladder*) You take that end. Come on, heave ho… (*Jean and Mrs Creggan get hold of the quite large ladder, get it upright and, mostly through Jean's efforts, positioned against the wall*). No, love, get it right at the end here – that's where blockage is.

They get the ladder manoeuvred into position.

Mrs Creggan shins up the ladder like a Houdini. At the top she fiddles about in the guttering.

MRS CREGGAN Mrs Darblay.

JEAN Yes.

MRS CREGGAN There's some'at stuck down here. I think it's one of those darn kids' tennis balls. Go into the kitchen and get me a large spoon. That'll do the trick.

The camera zooms in on Jean standing by ladder, impatience growing.

JEAN Yes, love.

Jean heads off into kitchen. From outside we can see her looking for a suitable spoon. Then there comes a scream from Mrs Creggan, and another, longer, scream. She has fallen with the ladder.

Jean comes out of the kitchen door as if shot from a cannon, and rushes to where Mrs Creggan is laid out moaning.

JEAN Are you all right?

MRS CREGGAN (*weak*) Ambulance. (*Jean makes a careful examination*) Doctor…

JEAN Don't move, love.

MRS CREGGAN Leg. Broke. It's broke. I know it.

Mrs Creggan goes into hysterical tears.

JEAN Just lie there, I'll get blankets – and an ambulance.

The camera focusses on Jean's face as she gets up – a picture of defeat.

11 The desk area at Hartley Police Station

Parrish is sitting at a table distinctly unhappy.

The phone rings: he answers it.

PARRISH Sir. Right away, sir.

He stands, checks his tunic and brushes his sleeves and tunic front with his hand before making for the Inspector's office.

He knocks on the door.

12 Jean's office

Robins is seated behind the desk.

The filing basket has been pushed to the front of the desk. The papers in it are disarranged and lie in all directions. Robins has clearly examined them and replaced them just as they fell, unconcerned that some hang over the sides.

ROBINS (*as Parrish enters*) Sergeant, I have finished my examination of these papers. (*He settles back in the chair. He is obviously going to enjoy this.*) Tell me, are you familiar with Fowler's English Usage?

PARRISH No, sir, not really familiar, sir.

ROBINS You should make yourself familiar with it, Sergeant. In fact, I'd like to hear that by the end of the week you've bought yourself the paperback edition of it. It's an invaluable guide to English grammar and the correct use of words. (*He indicates the filing basket of reports.*) Many of those reports forwarded by you contain basic errors in grammar and phraseology. For example; it is totally incorrect for a police officer, or anyone else for that matter, to say, "I was stood on the street corner"; it is, "I was standing on the street corner", and so on.

PARRISH (*in a last attempt at defiance*) I think, sir, that it's a question of background – everybody round here says, "I was stood on the corner" and the lads talk, I mean speak, the same way. With respect, sir, the Force Standing Orders say that Supervising Officers should not alter or reject reports because they do not agree with their phraseology, providing the meaning is clear. I don't think that you can fault any of the reports I have forwarded on those grounds.

ROBINS (*after allowing Parrish's protest to evaporate into silence*) A Supervisory Officer should take every opportunity to improve the standards of those supervised, and sloppy local dialects are to be deplored, particularly when they are used as an excuse for ignorance. Next... (*He picks up a horizontal duplicate book and starts to turn over the pages*)... I want to see all property which is in our possession and check it against these records.

PARRISH (*confidently because he knows*) You'll find it satisfactory, sir.

ROBINS Will I? I hope so. I'm going out to visit the patrols – when I return have ready for me all your sub-divisional records. Instruct CID for someone to be in that office at fourteen hundred hours. I shall wish to examine their records also.

Robins exits. Parrish collects the filing basket.

13 Outside Mrs Creggan's house

The camera shows us ambulance men wheeling Mrs Creggan, moaning, on a stretcher down the path out of her house to the back of an ambulance. Jean is following.

MRS CREGGAN Wait! Wait.

The two ambulance men have halted anyway, prior to opening the rear doors of the ambulance.

MRS CREGGAN Mrs Darblay.

JEAN Yes, love?

Mrs Creggan, horizontal, is fishing in her handbag which she's clutching to her stomach.

MRS CREGGAN You'll have to look after my Jack while I'm in hospital.

JEAN You may be all right, it might just be badly bruised.

MRS CREGGAN No, no. It's broken. I know it's broken. But you're my angel of mercy and you'll look after my Jack. It's a good job you're on holiday with nought to do.

JEAN (*flat*) I'm trying to decorate the front room, Mrs Creggan.

MRS CREGGAN See my Jack gets his meals. Do the shopping. (*Mrs Creggan pulls out a huge shopping list*) Pay for it. I'll refund when I'm feeling better.

Jean's looking at the list.

JEAN (*sharp*) There are near fifty items on this list.

MRS CREGGAN Week's shopping. Everything from Co-op, please. Now I mean that, 'cos Jack won't eat his gammon steak unless it's the Co-op. You'll have to do this now, love. He has his gammon every Monday night. Never misses.

JEAN (*despair*) I'm trying to decorate the front room, Mrs Creggan.

MRS CREGGAN (*ignoring*) And his tea is prompt at six. He'll take no excuse.

The ambulance men push Mrs Creggan on the stretcher into the ambulance.

MRS CREGGAN … And don't get me into trouble with it being late. Fry the gammon very slow, not crispy. And he likes his cauli done to a mush…

The ambulance men close the doors. One salutes Jean as they go round and get into their cab. The ambulance drives off. Jean standing there holding the long list of fifty items of the week's shopping. The camera zooms in on her.

JEAN Hells bells.

14   Inside a police car in Hartley

The police car is parked in a side road, about twenty yards from the junction with the main road.

Sitting in the driver's seat is PC Shelton, a good-looking young copper, well meaning, reasonably efficient but often gets a bit flustered for no good reason. He's writing a report on a clipboard on his knee, having difficulty sorting out his words.

The top button of his tunic is undone. He reads the report thus far as he does so, takes off his uniform cap and places it on the passenger seat.

SHELTON (*quietly to himself*) The road at this point is six metres wide and there is a broken white line marking the centre of the carriageway. The road bends gently to the left...

While he is reading, the camera pans back. A Ford Cortina can be seen travelling slowly along the side road. It pulls in directly behind Shelton's car.

The Cortina, immaculately cleaned and polished, is driven by Inspector Robins. We see his point of view momentarily through the back window of Shelton's car.

SHELTON ... From the point marked "A" on the plan, the driver of the Morris Marina, registration number... (*Shelton looks up from his report casually, into the driver's mirror. He sees Robins in car behind*) Oh, hell.

He quickly throws the clipboard onto the passenger seat, recovers his cap and crams it onto his head, in his haste almost completely covering his eyes and gets out of the car, all in one movement.

The camera moves to Robins's point of view again. Shelton can be seen tumbling out of the door of the car and coming towards the Cortina.

After he has walked two or three paces he realises that the door of the car has stayed wide open. He stops, returns, closes the door.

He then walks back to Robins, pulling his tunic down as he does so. Robins has remained in his car.

Shelton arrives at the Cortina driver's door, salutes, then bends forward.

SHELTON Sir.

The camera continues from Robin's view point, now focussing on the top button of Shelton's tunic which is unfastened. We see that one of his breast buttons is also unfastened.

ROBINS (*coldly and quietly*) Dress yourself. Properly.

Shelton tries to fasten both of his tunic buttons using both hands at once. Then for some reason he makes a quick check on his fly buttons.

ROBINS Your cap is to be worn at all times while on outside duty. This is your first and last warning. The next time you will be reported for disciplinary proceedings. I shall record this as an official caution on my return to the Station.

Robins extends his hand through the car window.

ROBINS Pocket book.

Shelton unfastens his tunic breast pocket, extracts his pocket book and hands it over, open.

Robins takes it from him without a word, examines it.

ROBINS The handwriting is appalling. Is this the best you can do?

SHELTON I do better when I'm sitting at a desk sir, but I did that stood up.

ROBINS Standing up, Constable, standing up. Your grammar is as deplorable as your handwriting. (*He initials the book, closes it and starts to return it. As he does so, a photograph slips out of the book.*

Robins picks it up and we see that it's of an attractive young woman.) And what is this?

SHELTON (*very confused*) It's my wife, sir.

ROBINS So you use your official pocket book as a gazeteer for your family snapshots. If this happens again, I shall have no alternative but to report you. Smarten yourself up!

He hands the pocket book back to Shelton. Before Shelton has the chance to say anything, Robins drives off.

15 The locker room in Hartley Police Station (evening)

Parrish can be seen steering Beck, like a conspirator, into the locker room. Beck's just come on shift and is clearly puzzled when Parrish closes the door.

BECK What is it, George?

PARRISH I'll tell you what it is – it's serious. Its name's Robins.

Inspector Robins. He's early thirties. Army background, I hear, fresh out of the College and about three weeks outside experience.

BECK Well?

PARRISH He's arrived like a ton of bricks. Never seen anything like it.

BECK We've had a relief Inspector before. God knows, Inspector Darblay, to us woman-haters, was a bit of a blow until we tamed her.

PARRISH Joe, this is different. This animal is out to get us. I know. This bloke wants me, certainly, and probably the whole bloody lot of us, on disciplinary proceedings by the end of the week.

BECK You?

PARRISH Yes, me.

BECK You don't mean it.

PARRISH I mean it!

BECK He can't put a whole bloody section on disciplinary proceedings.

PARRISH He can and he will. I don't mind myself – but I actually mind for Inspector Darblay. She comes back in a week and she finds three, four of her men on disciplinary charges, it's a reflection on her.

BECK Nobody would do that.

PARRISH He almost did it to Shelton today, and to me. And we're both on last warnings. He means it.

BECK Have you phoned Inspector Darblay about this?

PARRISH Of course not. And I won't. And don't you either. Look... (*on Beck, puzzled, thoughtful*) I've come up against people like this before. He walked in here. He took against the place, and I know he's got it in his mind to sort me out, or me and Shelton, or more. Now before that actually happens and it's too late to do anything about it, what are we going to do about him?

BECK Mr Lake?

PARRISH I don't think we can approach Mr Lake.

BECK Well, let me meet the bloke first. Then let me think about it.

PARRISH Does that mean, "Leave it to you to think about it and nothing will be done", or what?

BECK Let me tell you this. There's no bloody relief inspector's going to come into this section and take action against decent coppers like us for not crossing "ts" or dotting "is".

The door is pushed open, constables Shelton and Bentley enter. Bentley is carrying a pint bottle of milk.

BENTLEY Evening.

SHELTON (*to Beck*) Evening, Sarge. Did Inspector Darblay speak to you about duties this week?

BECK You're down for Three Area tonight.

SHELTON Magic, Sarge. Thanks. It should only be till Wednesday. Then her mother's coming to stay.

BECK Just three nights then, let me know if there's any change.

Shelton and Bentley breeze off. As they exit there is some playful jostling, Bentley tipping Shelton's helmet off.

PARRISH (*to Beck*) What's that about Three Area?

BECK Shelton's wife due any time. You know they're up the tops, at edge of town. It's very isolated up there. They've no telephone. If his wife needs help during the night she'll switch on their front bedroom light – you can see the window from pretty well all over Three Area. If he sees the light on he knows that things are happening.

(*Beck suddenly stops, stiffens, as Robins walks straight into the locker room*) Good evening, sir. I'm Joe Beck. I'm night sergeant this week. I don't think we've met.

ROBINS (*ignoring Beck*) Sergeant Parrish. I've just been in the billiard room – it's a disgrace. Before the shift goes off duty, be sure it's tidied up. If we must have cards and dominoes played in there, I want everything put away and the ashtrays emptied before it's left. (*turns to Beck*) I won't be at your briefing parade. But I shall be back later. Make sure that you and your men are on the ball.

Robins leaves the room

Beck and Parrish exchange glances

PARRISH There you are, what did I tell you!

16 The Darblays front room (night)

The camera shows us Jean wielding a roller.
She's just about got one wall done.
We hear the sound of the front door opening, closing.

Tom walks in.

TOM Hullo.

JEAN Hullo.

TOM What's that mountain of shopping in the hall? Expecting your mother?

JEAN It's not ours. It's Mrs Creggan's.

TOM (*matter-of-factly studying the paintwork*) You haven't done much.

JEAN (*angrily, despair in her voice*) D'you know what I've put up with today? Every twenty minutes an interruption. Mrs Creggan fell off a ladder. (*Tom laughs*) It's not funny. Had to get an ambulance, then do her week's shopping, then go visit her in hospital. And she's only going to be there over-night. No bones broken – God knows how – if you dropped that woman off the Empire State Building she'd bounce. She'll be back next door tomorrow. And she says, quote, she'll be asking me to run a few little errands – that's between the time I'll be doing meals on wheels for Mrs Maudsley. And then I had to cook her Jack his gammon steak, and I think I burned it. Anyhow, he took one look at it and he wouldn't eat it.

TOM What is all this?

JEAN Day one of my holiday!

TOM (*after a pause while he good-humouredly lets her simmer down*) Sweetheart, you said you wanted to do all this. You said it'd be therapeutic, relaxing.

JEAN (*a little mollified*) All right. All right.

TOM (*again gently*) Now all I want, darling, is some ale, some nosh, and my feet up. I've been five hours in the old folks home – all of it listening to complaints, complaints, complaints. I don't really need more of it when I come home.

JEAN All right. There's a shepherd's pie, warming up in the oven.

TOM You've eaten?

JEAN I've eaten.

TOM I'll give you some help with the painting after.

JEAN Thanks.

TOM Is that that new plastic paint you're using?

JEAN (*cagey*) Yes?

TOM Good stuff.

17 The locker room (night)

Parrish is sitting there in civilian clothes.
Beck enters, looks out in the corridor before closing the door behind him.

BECK (*angrily, quietly*) Okay, I've just spent half an hour with him – he's been checking the stationery cupboard. He got me to count the envelopes. He's a nut all right.

PARRISH So what do you suggest?

BECK We're going to think.

PARRISH Yes, well I've done a bit of that and I reckon the only thing we can do is to be so on the ball that he can't do us for anything.

BECK And that's the wrong approach.

PARRISH So what's the right one?

BECK Listen, in my long experience...

PARRISH Here we go, nowhere.

BECK In my many years I've learnt certain things. One of them is that there are always reasons why a bloke goes around behaving like a martinet, bawling the odds, trying to make himself out bigger and better than anyone else. There's always a reason for it. And the reason is often a weakness, like he's a closet alcoholic, or he likes ladies' clothes and when you can find that out you've got him.

18 The desk area

It's later the same night. Beck is on telephone, speaking quietly, hand over mouthpiece conspiratorially.
In the background the wall clock reads eleven-thirty.

BECK (*into telephone*) Wally, it's Joe Beck...I know the time... I expect you have just gone to bed...Quiet and listen! ... Personal records at Headquarters, that's down to you Wally...Listen comrade...got a bit of a problem I need your personal, confidential help on...

19 Outside Mrs Creggan's house (day)

We watch Jean balancing a tray containing a demolished lunch come out of the front door of Mrs Creggan's house, down the path, and round to start to move towards her own house. Suddenly the second floor bedroom window of the Creggans' house is thrown open. Mrs Creggan, on crutches, leans out.

MRS CREGGAN Me laundry at two-thirty, Mrs Darblay, don't forget.

JEAN (*grim*) No, Mrs Creggan.

MRS CREGGAN And you'll have to let doctor in to me at two.

JEAN You said that.

MRS CREGGAN Don't forget.

JEAN No, Mrs Creggan.

MRS CREGGAN And the milk for the cat.

20   The Darblays' front room

There's still one wall painted.
Jean crosses, still grim, to the paint pots. She opens one, stirs it, and starts to pour it into tray.

JEAN (*out loud*) Ladies and gentlemen, I'd like first to thank you sincerely for your invitation to speak to you tonight.... speak before you tonight...be with you tonight, which gives me the opportunity, the opportunity to a serving law officer to say some words on a subject of importance to me and importance in my work, the subject of the Children and Young Persons Act 1969... (*She's poured paint into tray and has put the paint roller in when the doorbell rings*). I don't believe it...

She exits to the hall.

21   Jean's hall

Jean opens the front door to reveal Parrish.

PARRISH 'Morning, ma'am.

JEAN George – what brings you here?

PARRISH Got some expenses for you, ma'am – just thought as I was passing I'd drop them in.

JEAN That's very kind of you, George.

PARRISH Pleasure, ma'am. How's the decorating going?

JEAN Slowly.

PARRISH Always the best way ma'am.

Jean senses Parrish is not just passing by and feels obliged to invite him in.

JEAN Come in, George – see if you approve of my "do-it-your-self" efforts.

PARRISH Well – thank you, ma'am.

Jean leads the way to the front room.

JEAN There, what do you think of that?

PARRISH Very nice, ma'am – you've nearly finished.

JEAN I've painted one wall, George – the object of the exercise is to paint the remaining three...

PARRISH I see... I thought... Well...

JEAN What's the matter, George – is everything okay?

PARRISH Yes of course, ma'am.

JEAN Oh come off it. You didn't drop in here just to pay me my expenses and admire the paintwork. What's the trouble?

PARRISH Well, ma'am – this relief Inspector Robins. He's upsetting things a bit.

JEAN Upsetting things?

PARRISH Well, he's giving me and Joe Beck a bit of pain and chasing the lads rotten. It's difficult, you know. We sympathise with the lads but we can't let them see it, or it'll really get out of hand. If he goes on, one of the lads is going to step right out of line, they'll only stand so much...

JEAN What is all this?

PARRISH I hear there's a move afoot for the lads to send a deputation to Mr Lake.

JEAN (*firmly*) Now you put a stop to that.

PARRISH You know what a close lot they are here – you kick one and they all limp...this Robins...

JEAN You mean *Inspector* Robins.

PARRISH Yes, ma'am, sorry, Inspector Robins – he's totally unreasonable, nit-picking and supercilious. I'm just worried that you're going to come back and find maybe two or three of us facing disciplinary proceedings.

JEAN Don't be ridiculous.

PARRISH I'm not, ma'am. And I'm just worried that Joe Beck is going to overstep the mark, because he's up to something with regard to this Robins, and I don't know what it is...

JEAN I don't want to hear any of this. I rely on you two sergeants to run the section for me. You are the supervisors. Get some supervising done. Cope.

PARRISH Yes, ma'am – sorry to have disturbed you –

JEAN That's perfectly all right, George – and since you're here, perhaps you could give me a hand to shift this lot.

141

She indicates the furniture which is up against the next wall she intends to paint.

PARRISH Right, Ma'am.

22 Inside a pub (early evening)

WALTERS (*miffed*) I've been going round making discreet and confidential enquiries on your behalf. On top of that, why am I buying you a drink?

BECK Consolation, Wally, for not coming up with much more than I could have found out myself.

WALTERS Now you didn't expect me to secrete Maurice Albert Robins's personal file out of our Records under my mac for you to spill your beer on.

BECK Hardly.

WALTERS And I don't want it to get back to Personnel Department that any crumb of knowledge you may acquire came from a discreet Headquarters Sergeant like me.

BECK You must have changed. All right – so what have we got so far? What about school? Where did he go?

WALTERS St Marks, Oldham. Left with three "O" levels.

BECK Only three!

WALTERS How many have you got?

BECK I don't put on airs and graces, Wally. Three "O" levels, and he told George Parrish to buy some grammar book.

WALTERS He would. He's been that long in admin. and training – he's forgotten what operational work's all about.

BECK Well I wish he hadn't been parked on us as a reminder. So what about his army service?

WALTERS Five years – South Yorkshire Regiment. Rank full Sergeant.

BECK That's a turn up.

WALTERS What's wrong?

BECK What's wrong? His bloody airs and graces again. You'd expect him to be a short-term commissioned officer. Not a loud-mouthed sergeant.

WALTERS So?

BECK I don't know. You're not helping me, Wally. What about his army record?

WALTERS How would he get into the Force if there was anything shown to his detriment? Hang on. Just had a thought.

BECK What?

WALTERS When a chap leaves the Army he's given a character grading... Exemplary, Very good, Good, etc....

BECK So?

WALTERS Well, your Inspector Robins on discharge was only described as "very good".

BECK Yeah, well?

WALTERS Well, if he was so flaming marvellous – why wasn't he rated "exemplary"...?

BECK Ah! You might have a point there. I'll have a word with Eddie Cullen. He's an old soldier. Perhaps he knows somebody in the South Yorkshire Regiment who can tell me about Maurice Albert Robins.

23   Outside the Sheltons' house

Shelton is seen leaving for work. He wheels his bicycle out of the gate, and is seen off by a very pregnant wife.

SHELTON Ta'ra luv. Take care...and get some rest.

MRS SHELTON Don't worry, love. I'll be all right.

SHELTON I'll try and look in sometime during the evening, same as usual.

MRS SHELTON Ta'ra love.

SHELTON Ta'ra.

He cycles away down the lane.

24   Jean's office Hartley Police Station

Robins is seated at the desk writing in a pocket book. There is a knock at the door.

ROBINS Enter.

Sergeant Beck enters.

BECK You wanted to see me, sir?

ROBINS That's right, Sergeant. I've been checking the Parade States and the Disposition sheets. (*He hands Beck two or three sheets of paper.*) You'll see I've made some changes – I noticed that this is the third night in succession that PC Shelton has been allocated Three Area. You know, or you ought to know, Sergeant, it's bad policing and bad supervision to put the same man on the same area repeatedly.

It can lead to slackness, or even worse. I've transferred Shelton to foot patrol in the town centre.

BECK About Shelton, sir. I don't know if you know, but his wife's expecting a baby, and it's any minute now, and Inspector Darblay left instructions that...

ROBINS Inspector Darblay is on leave. I'm in charge of this station. You follow *my* instructions without question or argument – is that clear? Constable Shelton will patrol the town centre on foot – that is all, Sergeant.

BECK Yes sir.

25 The locker room

Five constables are present, including Shelton and Bentley. Beck has a clipboard in his hand:
It's the night shift briefing. The parade is part way through.
Inspector Robins stands behind Beck, radiating disapproval.

BECK Seven one eight nine?

BENTLEY Sarge?

BECK (*very formal*) You're on Two and Three Areas, I'll give you a call later on. There's a couple of pubs up there that are due a visit closing time, I'll arrange a meet with you – and keep an eye on that vulnerable property on the edge of Three Area – any lights or unusual activity give us a call, you know the drill.

BENTLEY Right, Sarge. I'll keep an eye on it.

BECK (*to Robins*) Anything else, sir?

ROBINS No, fall them out.

BECK (*to men*) Right, fall out.

Robins exits.
Beck crosses to Shelton.

BECK I thought the bit about your missus as the vulnerable property on the edge of Three Area was quite bloody brilliant...

SHELTON Much appreciated, Sarge.

BECK Spread the word around, lad. I don't want anybody getting into trouble tonight because I've got to slip away on a private matter to do with all our futures, and I don't want the balloon going up and me found missing.

SHELTON I'll spread the word, Sarge.

BECK In a whisper, lad.

SHELTON Right, Sarge.

BENTLEY (*to Shelton as the men leave*) After that you should make Sergeant Beck godfather.

26 Outside the Sheltons' house

The house is in long shot, on the brow of the hill. The curtains are drawn and all is dark. Then suddenly the bedroom curtains are pulled apart – and the light shines out.
We cut to a town alleyway where Shelton is walking along, shining his torch into recesses and alleyways.

27 A banquet hall ante-room (the same night)

The camera takes in a caption by the door: Hartley Law Society.
A bored porter stands by the door reading the "Sporting Pink".
Laughter can be heard – then Jean's voice.

JEAN ... Seriously, this is a problem which we all face, ladies and gentlemen.

28 Inside the banquet hall

We are concentrating on a small section of the top table. Jean, in evening gown, is standing. We catch sight of Tom, seated next to Jean – and the chairman.

JEAN I would ask you to make the strongest representations through your various professional associations to have this bad law changed. (*This provokes calls of Hear, Hear, and scattered applause*) I hope, Mr President, that I haven't abused your hospitality by riding this particular hobby-horse on this occasion, but it's not often we women have the chance to make ourselves heard. (*laughter, Jean smiles*) May I say again, thank you for inviting us to join you at your Society's Annual Dinner. The Hartley Law Society has every reason to be proud of the professional standards maintained by its members – I commend you all for this and thank you.

Jean sits down to warm applause.

29   A town shopping street

Shelton is still checking shop doors.

30   We cut to the Sheltons' house

The light shines. The night is silent.

31   and back to the town shopping street

A police car drives up, pulls in beside Shelton. It's driven by Bentley, who gestures to him. Shelton crosses, opens the passenger door.

SHELTON What's up then?

BENTLEY The light's gone on in your house. Get in quick.

SHELTON I'll have to be back in case Mr Robins comes checking.

BENTLEY Come on. Get in. I called ambulance.

Shelton gets in, slams the door and the police car roars away.

As it drives off the camera pans to a shop doorway on the other side of the road. Inspector Robins steps out of the doorway, takes out his pocket book, makes an entry and then replaces it in his tunic pocket. His expression says it all: Shelton is for it.

We follow the police car travelling fast.

SHELTON ...typical of a woman – never on time for anything. Probably be a false alarm when we get there... (*then more apprehensive*) I hope everything's okay, Roland. If we run across any bosses on the way, we're right up the creek.

The radio crackles

PARRISH (*voice distorted*) Hartley to seven one eight nine.

BENTLEY Oh lor..

SHELTON You're stuck with me now. Answer the man.

BENTLEY Seven-one-eight-nine to Hartley.

32   The radio room

Parrish is seen at the radio control

PARRISH (*voice distorted*) Seven one eight nine. Go to the Co-op on Ridgeway Road. A Mrs Dodsworthy of seventy-nine The Rise thinks she saw a torch flashing in the shop. Investigate and report.

BENTLEY Will do, Sarge. Seven one eight nine. Out.

BENTLEY Shall I drop you?

SHELTON What's the point. I should be in town. Roland – you
did call an ambulance, didn't you?

BENTLEY Yes I did.

The car changes direction.

We cut quickly to the Sheltons' house.

The light shines on in the silence.

And back to a road behind a Co-op store.

*The police car pulls up. Bentley and Shelton get out quietly, shut the car
doors quietly, approach the front of the shop, examine the door and move
away to go round the back.*

33   The Co-op shop's rear storeroom

*The storeroom is piled high to the ceiling with cardboard boxes of goods,
everything from Persil to Kit-E-Kat. The Richards brothers, Harry and
Jack, well-known local villains, burst into the room.*

HARRY What are we going to do?

JACK Only two of them? You sure?

HARRY Yes. What do we do?

JACK Keep bloody quiet and hope they'll scarper.

HARRY They'll not do that.

Pan with them to back of shelves.

34   Back of the Co-op

*Bentley and Shelton arrive at the door to the storeroom and find the broken
handle.*

35   The storeroom

Harry and Jack are watching from behind a shelving unit.

HARRY What about the front of the shop?

JACK I told you – front door's dead-locked. I checked it yesterday.

HARRY Then we're bloody trapped...

JACK Two against two – you've got to be joking...shh...

From their point of view we see Bentley and Shelton cautiously enter the storeroom. Shelton remains by the doorway as Bentley cautiously moves into the room. Meanwhile Jack and Harry, using the piled goods as cover, work their way towards Shelton – and escape. Harry, inevitably, trips over some object. All hell breaks loose and after a fierce struggle the two villains are overpowered – a fair amount of mayhem having been caused in the process.

BENTLEY (*breathless, tightening his grip on Harry*) Well, you recognise this lot then..

SHELTON (*breathless now that Jack is trapped underneath his weight*) ...Richards brothers.

BENTLEY Right. Well known. And well wanted.

They exchange wide, pleased grins.

36   The Sheltons' house

The light continues to shine, but the silence is broken as from a distance an ambulance can be heard and seen approaching.

37   The banquet hall ante-room (night)

Jean and Tom are now collecting their coats, before leaving.

JEAN What did you think of it?

TOM I really enjoyed it.

JEAN So did I.

TOM Your mum would be proud of you. It's quiet an achievement.

JEAN What's that?

TOM I don't know – from raw recruit, years ago, to now, lecturing the lawyers of the Hartley Law Society on what is what.

JEAN Don't say how many years ago or I'll hit you with my handbag.

TOM Yes, dear.

The bored porter comes up to Jean. He hands her a note.

JEAN Thanks. (*inspects note*) George Parrish...letting me know young Shelton's wife's been rushed into hospital...the baby's on its way. Do you mind, Tom?

TOM Home by way of the office?

JEAN You read me like a book. (*thinking aloud*) Joseph should be on duty tonight. What's George Parrish doing on duty?

38 The desk area Hartley Police Station

Jean, Tom, Shelton and Bentley clustered around Parrish, who's sitting at a typewriter, telephone in hand, helping the two young cops get out their report.

PARRISH Right. CID on their way. What a good do. The brothers know they're bang to rights. And now one of our heroes here (*indicates Shelton*) is about to produce another example of his virility and aggression. (*The phone rings. Parrish picks it up.*) Yes. Hartley Cottage Hospital. Hang on. (*hands the phone to Shelton*) For you, lad.

SHELTON (*into the phone*) Constable Ian Shelton speaking. I see. Well, thank you very much. Is she okay? Yes, well, will you please give her my love. (*He replaces phone, looking stunned and in a flat tone tells the group.*) I've got a son.

They all react:
Bentley lets out a shriek,
Jean gets up and kisses Shelton,
Parrish pumps his hand,
Tom slaps him on the back.

TOM Bloody well done.

JEAN Congratulations, Ian. Well done. How is she? Did they say how much he weighs?

We focus on Shelton's face still stunned.

SHELTON (*quietly*) Excuse me. ...I'm a bit...overcome. D'you mind...well, I'd...I'd like to go somewhere...and just sit with meself private like, do you mind?

JEAN Of course.

The cheers tail off to silence.

Shelton wanders unsteadily over to corridor, and exits.

BENTLEY He wants to be by himself.

PARRISH He's a dad. I know how he feels. It'll be like winning the football pools – tonight. And losing the cheque – tomorrow.

JEAN (*to Tom*) I think it's our cue to go.

TOM Goodnight, everybody.

JEAN (*to Bentley*) Terrific job, getting the Richards brothers. Top marks. (*to Parrish*) Goodnight, George.

PARRISH Goodnight, ma'am. Goodnight, Tom.

BENTLEY Goodnight, ma'am. Mr Darblay.

JEAN (*as she and Tom exit*) Keep up the good work, Roland.

PARRISH (*to Bentley*) All right then. Let's get on with this report.

BENTLEY What about Shelton?

PARRISH Give him half hour with his thoughts. There is a time when a man wants to be alone with himself.

BENTLEY A man? Shelton a *man*?

PARRISH (*quotes*) "We arrived at the Ridgeway Road premises of the Hartley Co-operative..."

Robins enters.

Strides in.

ROBINS (*controlled anger*) Where is Constable Shelton?

PARRISH Locker room, sir. He's just learned by phone that he's the father of a baby boy... And I am pleased to inform you, sir, that Bentley here and Shelton have caught a well known pair of local villains.

ROBINS Bentley – I am taking disciplinary proceedings against you and PC Shelton for deliberately absenting your-selves from your beats, a most serious infringement of orders, which I personally witnessed.

PARRISH If I may say in their defence, sir they told me they...temporarily absented...

ROBINS Bentley, find Shelton and report to my office immedi-ately.

BENTLEY Yes, sir. (*He goes*)

ROBINS And why are you on duty? Where is Sergeant Beck?

PARRISH He phoned me to come in and cover. He has to deal with a very unexpected and urgent family matter, sir.

Robins exits to the office.

39 A corner of a Sergeants' mess (the same night)

Beck is seated at a table.

With him, in army Sergeant's uniform, is Sergeant Joel, in charge of South Yorkshire Regiment records.

The two men are relaxed and deep in conversation.

JOEL So you're a mate of Eddie Cullen's?

BECK Yeah.

JOEL How is he now?

BECK Well, he's bought his second shop. Must be doing well.

JOEL Bright lad.

BECK Nice man.

JOEL Eddie said you were inquiring about Sergeant Robins.

BECK Yeah.

JOEL Well you've come to the right man. I've heard of that one, all right. He's well known in the folklore of the South Yorkshires.

BECK Maurice Albert Robins?

JOEL That's the one. I've checked. But I remember the Robins story.

BECK What Robins story?

JOEL Sergeant Robins was five years with us. Left six years ago. He was a right tartar. There are squaddies who still remember him, will always remember him.

BECK Remember what?

JOEL Well, he was a strict disciplinarian; played everything by the book; never put a foot out of line, but was never one of the lads. And then literally, literally two days before his demob, he went to some party, got blind drunk and ended up fast asleep lying flat out on a pedestrian crossing on the Barnsley Road. And when the MPs came to collect him, he had a right go at them.

BECK He did that?

JOEL There were a lot of blokes who were highly delighted by that escapade I can tell you.

BECK I'm quite pleased to hear about it myself.

40 Jean's front room (day)

The radio is playing. Jean by now "into the swing" of painting, has only the window wall to complete. She seems to be cheerful.

41 Jean's office

Bright sunlight pours through the windows to reveal Robins behind a neat pile of papers on the desk. There's a knock on the door.

ROBINS Enter.

(*Beck enters*)

BECK Good morning, sir.

ROBINS Yes, Sergeant Beck?

BECK A word with you, sir.

ROBINS Concerning your "unexpected" absence from duty last night I presume.

BECK I hear you are considering disciplinary proceedings against Constables Shelton and Bentley, and that you intend to put these into effect this morning.

ROBINS What business is this of yours?

BECK Shelton had his first child last night.

ROBINS So I understand.

BECK And they also caught the Richards brothers.

ROBINS Yes I am aware of that.

BECK I wish to make a plea on their behalf before you take official action against them.

ROBINS (*snaps*) You're wasting your time, sergeant, and mine. That is all.

BECK No, you will hear me out, sir.

ROBINS Are you disobeying my orders?

BECK Yes, sir. We all make mistakes from time to time in our lives. To err is human, sir.

ROBINS Leave this office.

BECK I was only hearing last night the story of a sergeant in the South Yorkshire Regiment who had an exemplary army career until two days before his demob when, uncharacteristically, he got very drunk and lay down on a pedestrian crossing and then gave aggro to some MPs who came to collect him. (*as Beck talks we see a series of reaction shots: Robins, then Beck, then Robins, to Beck's blank face, to Robins's as Robins's expression changes slowly from white fury to complete defeat.*) It was a story told to me in confidence and of course will not go further around the force. I think on reflection, inspector, these are very young lads, and you should be able to see your way clear to letting them off with a verbal warning. I think that would be the wisest course. Don't you agree, sir?

ROBINS (*after a long pause*) Tell them to report to me at eleven hundred hours.

BECK Thank you, sir.

Beck turns and goes.

The camera moves in to hold Robins's face in defeat.

42 Jean's front room

The window wall is finished and Jean is now painting the door.

43 Lake's office at District Headquarters (evening)

Lake is seated behind desk smoking a pipe.
Robins is standing facing him across the desk, without hat or gloves.

ROBINS Yes, a most rewarding week at Hartley, sir. One has to adapt to a semi-rural situation. The staff are very sound. The younger men impressed me with their keenness and reliability. I tightened a few things up – not that Inspector Darblay had let things go, but – well, you know how it is, sir, we men do it differently.

LAKE Differently doesn't always mean better. From what I hear you haven't created a very good impression during the last week for either man-management or tact. You've a long way to go in the service, Maurice. If you take my advice, you'll unbend a bit. If you don't, it's going to be a long, hard and lonely road for you. Good luck to you.

ROBINS *(after a pause)* Thank you, sir.

44 The Darblays' front room (evening)

We see Jean standing there, paint brush in hand, surveying her work – the room is finished.

JEAN Tom.

TOM *(off vision)* Finished?

JEAN Yes.

Tom walks in, a sandwich in one hand, mug of tea in the other.

JEAN Mind the door – it's still wet.

Tom looks around.

There's silence from Jean, and we have the sense that she's going to pounce on him if he utters one word of criticism.

TOM Terrific job. What about the ceiling?

JEAN What about it?

TOM Are you going to paint it?

JEAN *(sharp)* I've painted four walls not to mention the woodwork, while the world collapsed in chaos around me, and that's it. That's the end of "do-it-yourself" for me, for life.

TOM I would have thought it was more logical to get the ceiling painted before the walls – I mean, paint from the ceiling is now going to splash on your new painted walls.

JEAN Why the hell didn't you mention it before?

TOM Didn't sort of look as though it needed doing before, if you know what I mean.

JEAN (*after a long hard silence*) I don't care.

TOM What d'you mean, you don't care?

JEAN I phoned Joseph Beck's pal, John Oakley. Decorator, capenter. He came. He looked upstairs. He starts on Monday.

TOM Does he? What's he going to charge?

JEAN Seventy-five pounds a room excluding paint. And after what I've been through, that's cheap.

TOM (*noncommittal*) Oh.

JEAN It's the weekend. I've got forty-eight hours of leave left. Take me to Blackpool.

TOM But I hate Blackpool.

JEAN What do you mean, *you* hate Blackpool? *I* hate Blackpool. But compared with what I've been through these past five days, Blackpool is suddenly heaven. All right?

TOM All right.

JEAN (*ordering*) Go pack your toothbrush. I'll phone an hotel. Now.

TOM Yes, Inspector Darblay…

He wanders out. Jean takes up the paint roller, in its tray and goes over to a large tea chest. It contains all the rubbish, the empty paint tins and newspapers from her painting spree. With a gesture of finality she adds the roller and tray.

Points for Discussion and Suggestions for Writing

Shot Gun

1 Jean has been in Hartley fourteen days when Superintendent Lake asks her, "How are the lot taking it – a woman in charge?" What problems face Jean? Are they particularly those of a woman in a male-dominated environment, or are they problems that anyone new would experience when taking charge?

2 Adapting to a new boss is of course just as difficult as being the boss. What are the problems encountered by those under Jean's command? Do *you* react differently to having a woman in charge?

3 What do you think are the best ways of establishing authority? And the best ways of losing it!? As a class decide on a situation of someone establishing authority. Then in groups prepare dramatisations that demonstrate the different sequences that could follow.

4 Police work requires attention to a number of jobs going on at the same time. Jean is called away from the rape investigation. See if you can complete the case.

5 The episode doesn't have the traditional happy ending. Indeed, Jean blunders by waiting for Lake and maintaining a silence instead of a dialogue. Why does she then turn on Beck? What is the effect of this ending on him – and on us? Do you feel any sympathy for Jean?

6 Briefly describe the relationship between Jean and Tom as we know it so far.

7 After you've read the piece by Joan Clark, the Script Editor, (page ix), work out the "stock sets" and "regular characters" Ian Kennedy Martin had to use – i.e. the ones you think will appear in other episodes.

Coins

1. This episode is not a typical television drama about police work. Can you list the various events and types of action you have come to expect in a police series? How has Ray Jenkins broken the formula here, and yet given us an entertaining episode?

2 Building homes and shelters: everyone's at it in this episode. What are the reasons each individual would give for his or her activity? Do you think Major Adams is foolish preparing his shelter? Why do most people like – even need – a "place of my own"? Design and describe yours, actual or imaginary.

3 Why is Kenny special to Carol? Do you think adults often "jump to conclusions" about teenage friendships? What do you look for in a friend?

4 The other job that Jean is concerned with in this episode is restraining visiting football supporters. What do you think are the best methods the police can use (a) to prevent trouble and (b) in the event of trouble from and between supporters?

5 After you've read the piece by Ray Jenkins on script writing (page xii), decide how *you* would have concluded this episode.

Family Unit

1 Jennie says about this case, "The police concern is, Murphy beat up his daughter, might do it again, and has three other motherless children floating about. I can say I know John Murphy. I know he didn't beat Maeve because he hates her, or because he's mad or dangerous.... He's a kid himself." Now give the social services concern as briefly.

2 Think about the title of this episode and balance it against this quotation from the end – "a matter of principle". Could – or should – Tom have avoided appearing in court? Do you think Maeve should stop seeing the boy who upsets her father? Can you describe an occasion when you've had a conflict of loyalties?

3 After you've read what Ian Kennedy Martin has written about his approach to creating characters (page x), make the list he'd have prepared of Murphy's attitudes. Why does Murphy impress the magistrates? What do *you* think of him?

4 There are two episodes which concern batterings. Compare this case with that in *Expectations* and work out why each happened. Can you think of other reasons why one person batters another? What can be done to help?

5 Why are Jean and Tom "both losers"? How has their relationship changed since the first episode?

Expectations

1 This episode looks at two people new to their jobs. Consider Hannah first. What can *you* learn from her first days in the police force? Write some of the entries which might have appeared in her private diary covering this time.

2 What is Hannah trying to achieve by leaving the word "PIG" on her forehead? Why have the police been called this? How would you suggest the police could improve their relationship with the communities they serve?

3 We are given in this episode a very vivid picture of the work of a social work team. Has it changed your impression of social workers? How do you think Tom could have helped Laura and Jack?

4 Jennie says to Tom about social work "We're not in competition with each other ... It's not a job you can measure success in like that!" How then do you think social workers can measure success? Think of a range of other jobs and services, and work out how each determines success. If each type of work leads to its own individual result, why are some people considered "more successful" than others?

5 Why is Tom under stress? Write out the report his social worker might give if he had one! How can Jean help him?

6 Describe or dramatise an occasion on which you wanted to create a favourable impression – and failed. Why is it easier to present such a scene in a lighthearted style? Why isn't this episode produced that way?

Relief

1 How is Robins different to Jean in his approach to his job, his position, and the men? Look at some of the instructions he gives, and explain why he's "giving ... a bit of pain" to the men.

2 Mrs Creggan is also being bossy. Rewrite the dialogue between her and Jean, as the former is leaving for hospital, so that Jean's farewell words are "Now don't you worry. I'll do my best for Jack. You just look after yourself."

3 When Parrish complains to Jean about Robins, she's quite sharp with him. How do you think a person responsible for others should respond to complaints about his/her equal?

4 Robins says to Parrish: "It is totally incorrect for a police officer, or anyone else for that matter, to say 'I was stood on the street corner' ". What do you think of this statement? Would you respond in a different way if Beck, for instance, had said it?

5 "There're always reasons why a bloke goes around behaving like a martinet." What do you think of Beck's activities to bribe Robins? Would it have been "better" for Beck to have discussed the situation with Lake or Jean? We get the impression that Robins won't change as a result of this episode. What could be done to help him "unbend a bit"?

General Questions

1 Compare Jean with other police series heroes, British and American, male and female. You might like to draw up lists of attitudes, as Ian Kennedy Martin does, for some of them, and ask others in the class to guess which character you had in mind.

2 "Juliet Bravo" is a radio call-sign. Invent suitable call-signs for other police characters.

3 Why is the police drama such a popular programme on television today? What do you look for in a police series? What do police series do for the image of the police force? Do you think the police force has been misrepresented?

4 Arrange that all the class will watch the same police programme one evening, so that you can discuss some of the

points of production. If possible collect newspaper reviews of the programme to consider at the same time.

5 After considering what a TV critic writes about, prepare a short review of one of the episodes in this book. Half the class might like to write in praise, the other half in contempt of it!

6 How do you feel reading these episodes compares to seeing them on television?

The Scriptwriters

Ian Kennedy Martin

Leaving university without a degree, Ian Kennedy Martin joined the BBC as a staff writer in 1963. He had written two TV plays which the BBC had bought but did not produce. For the next few years he alternated script writing and TV story editing. "The more successful a writer you become, the more you're condemned to an empty and silent room. It's important to escape that isolation from time to time and meet people. TV story editing places you right in the middle of the mad-house of television production – and can be very creative." However, from 1967 onwards, Ian concentrated more on script writing for both BBC and ITV (with a sojourn in Hollywood working on film scripts). After this began a decade of contributions to a wide range of TV series. 'The Troubleshooters', 'Hadleigh', 'Colditz', 'The Onedin Line' were some of the hundred-and-fifty scripts written in this period.

In 1974 Ian created 'The Sweeney' for a close friend, the actor John Thaw. After 'The Sweeney' he turned to prose and wrote seven novels – among these, *Rekill and Billions*. After this prose interlude, Ian went back to television and created two new series for the BBC – 'Juliet Bravo' and 'The Chinese Detective'. The BBC plan to continue production of both these series in the future.

Ray Jenkins

Ray Jenkins was born in Oxford, went to school there, then to Trinity College, Cambridge, and then to Paris. Coming back from France and having no job, he took up teaching – first in a London Comprehensive and then in a Teachers' Training College. Then, he says, he gave up value to earn money, and since 1965 has written over 160 scripts for radio, film and theatre, plus a handful of books for children. Television series he has contributed to include 'This Man Craig', 'Callan', 'The Troubleshooters', 'Z Cars', 'The Main Chance', 'Justice', 'The Expert', 'The Sweeney', 'Target', 'Villains', 'The Brothers', 'Accident', and 'The Gentle Touch'.

Paula Milne

Paula Milne studied fine art at the Central School of Art and Design, and subsequently took a post-graduate course in film making at the Royal College of Art. In 1973 she joined the BBC as a script reader, and later became a script editor in the series/serial department, where she devised the original series of *Angels*. In 1976 she left the BBC to become a free lance writer. She has over forty television credits, and has contributed to such series as 'Coronation Street', 'Crown Court', 'Z Cars', 'Juliet Bravo', 'Rooms', 'The Foundation', 'Premier', 'Angels', 'A Bunch of Fives' and others. More recently she dramatised Kathleen Conlon's novel *My Father's House* is seven episodes for Granada Television and wrote a four-part love story for the BBC entitled 'Love is Old, Love is New'. She has also written two Plays for Today, a six-part teenage series for Thames television, and has just completed an original novel for Virago, called *John David*. She is thirty-four years old, and lives in North London with her husband and three young children.

Teachers' notes

It is an understatement to say that there is a lack of communication between the police and teenagers today, and as a result much misunderstanding on both sides. A teacher is well-placed to encourage an awareness of the dilemmas of policing society, and even to arrange a dialogue. The policemen and women at any local station will be pleased to receive such an invitation, and will no doubt organise a trip round the station in return for their visit into class.

I hope that the selection of scripts in this volume go some way, in any case, to uncover the cliche of the "human face of the law". Four of the scripts consider situations where young people "become involved" with the police. But it is worth pointing out that in two of them (*Shot Gun* and *Family Unit*) the role of the police is to protect the youngsters from an aggressive parent, and in only one of them (*Coins*) is the "involvement" taken as the central concern of the inspector and her staff. Two of the scripts (*Shot Gun* and *Relief*) look at another key issue for today's youth: the establishment and use of authority, but it is only in the latter that we see this authority misdirected. I believe that all this is a realistic reflection of the work of the police, but, whether you agree or not, it is obviously a suggestion worth discussing with a class.

Before I started work on this volume, I confess I knew little about police work, and would have felt reluctant to venture deep in discussions on the topic, especially with young adults in their years of rebellion. Teachers in a similar position might be interested in some of the books listed here. They come from the shelves of a police inspector who is in a similar position to Jean Darblay. They represent part of his professional reading and are given here, in order of interest, with his own comments.

Reference books

Scotland Yard: A Study of the Metropolitan Police by Peter Laurie (Penguin 1972) ISBN 0 14 00 3361 0
A very readable detailed summary of police work, it looks at all functions of police work on every level. It has a useful glossary and a good appendix on Judges' Rules, most of which is still up to date.
Spike Island: Portrait of a Police Division by James McClure (Pan 1980) ISBN 0 330 26278 5
A comprehensive look at the everyday life of the Merseyside police, in popular reportage style.
Policing Freedom: A Commentary on the Dilemmas of Policing in Western Democracies by John Alderson (MacDonald and Evans 1979) ISBN 0 7121 1815 2.
An idealistic book, but gives a model for discussion about community policing. There is a very far-ranging bibliography at the end of each chapter.
The Police We Deserve edited by J. C. Alderson and Philip John Stead (Wolfe 1973) ISBN 0 7234 0515 8
A series of short essays in a popularised intellectual style. A summary of the general discussion on principles that goes on over the years.
In the Office of Constable by Robert Mark
(Collins 1978) ISBN 0 00 216032 3
Autobiography of a past Commissioner of the Metropolitan Police.
A Policeman's Lot: A Collection of Police Humour compiled by G. A. Harris (Police Review Publishing Co 1980) ISBN 0 85164 993 9
An amusing collection.

****

The following might also be useful:
The Lawbreakers by Ray Jenkins
(Penguin Education 1968) ISBN 0 14 080089 1
A provocative collage of material specially designed for use in schools. *Teachers' Notes* on the Series (Connexions) has suggestions for further study.

Policeman's Progress by Harry Cole
(Fontana 1980) ISBN 0 00 635842 X
A Metropolitan policeman's experiences in the Southwark area,
of life on the beat in London.
British Policewoman: Her Story by Joan Lock
(Robert Hale 1979) ISBN 0 7091 7546 9
An entertaining historical account. The gradual steps in setting
up the women's police are traced through the two main and
very different campaigners.
Police – the monthly magazine of the Police Federation, avail-
able from their office, 15–17 Langley Road, Surbiton, Surrey
KT6 6LP.
Police Review – a weekly journal published on Fridays and
available from good newsagents.

Police fiction

*This selection of novels concerns young people who become involved in the world
of crime and the police.*

Ashley, B.	Kind of wild justice	O.U.P.	1978	19271417 1
Banks, L.R.	Writing on the wall	Chatto	1981	70112568 3
Bawden, N.	The robbers	Gollancz	1979	57502695 2
Brown, R.	Find Debbie	Penguin	1979	14047131 6
Burch, T.R.	Tigs crime	Collins	1981	00671748 9
Dhondy, F.	Siege of Babylon	Macmillan	1978	33323705 6
Dickinson, P.	Seventh raven	Gollancz	1981	57502960 9
Harvey, J.	What about it Sharon?	Penguin	1979	14047159 6
Hornsby, K.	Wet behind the ears	Dobson	1980	23472202 9
Jeffries, R.	Boy who knew too much	Penguin	1979	14031115 7
King, C.	Me and my million	Penguin	1979	14031128 9
Line, D.	Mike and me	Penguin	1976	14030784 2
Loxton, M.	The job	Longman	1977	58222159 5
Miles, P.	Disturbing influence	H. Hamilton	1978	24110022 4
Peyton, K.M.	Midsummer's night dream	O.U.P.	1978	19271422 8
Peyton, K.M.	Pennington's seventeenth summer	O.U.P.	1979	19277081 0
Rees, D.	Risks	Heinemann	1977	43495819 0
Savage, J.	Club hammer	Macmillan	1978	33324694 2
Storey, M.	Keep running	Penguin	1979	14031198 X
Tate, J.	Ginger Mick	Longman	1976	58223131 0